A Gardener's Progress

A
Gardener's Progress

by

Gwladys Tonge

Faber and Faber
London

First published in 1974
by Faber and Faber Limited
3 Queen Square London WC1
Printed in Great Britain by
Latimer Trend & Company Ltd Plymouth
All rights reserved

ISBN 0 571 10607 2

Acknowledgements

I am most grateful to Catherine Uren for her enthusiasm and encouragement, and for so patiently typing and retyping my manuscript.

I would also like to thank P. W. & L. Thompson Ltd., who took the colour photograph for the jacket and ten of the other photographs, and the *Coventry Evening Telegraph*, who allowed me to reproduce the illustration for plate number 1.

Gwladys Tonge

Contents

Illustrations

Introduction

 THIS IS NOT A MANUAL OF INSTRUCTION, NEITHER IS it a description by an expert of how a beautiful garden was created. It is merely the sharing of a very ordinary and unambitious amateur gardener's experience with anyone sufficiently interested to read these chapters. Some of my friends are really great gardeners. They have known and grown and loved many plants; and their knowledge and skill in cultivating so far exceeds mine that they should write of these, rather than I of my paltry horticultural progress. But they remain silent while I chatter on, and from the past hear once again the acid comment of a disapproving schoolmistress, that empty vessels make most sound!

I must record my thanks to those gardening friends who have roused my interest in this or that plant by their own love and enthusiasm for it, who have gladdened my heart and beautified my borders with generous gifts of plants, cuttings and seedlings. But an honourable mention must go also to the not-so-keen-on-gardening friends, and the fortitude with which they have tramped round my garden showing, as required, wonder, amazement and admiration at each plant and leaf about which I poured forth such a wealth of unwanted information. They could quite justifiably have used the following pungent little rhyme to silence me:

> You had a lovely garden, full of earth's fairest flowers.
> You walked me round and round it and vexed my
>   soul for hours.
> I hate your brown genista, I hate your cedar tree
> Yes, open up your vista, but what is that to me?
> May frost your borders harden, and slug and aphis too
> Destroy your lovely garden, your boiler house and you.

Perhaps the only real progress I can claim as a gardener is that I no longer offer to show people round the garden unless I feel sure they want to be shown — and I am learning to wait until they ask!

Writing about the gardens I admired as a child, I find it impossible not to use the purple prose by which alone I can describe the brilliance those gardens contained. Reading my descriptions, I am appalled at the difficulty of painting accurately the picture I still see so clearly, and of conveying the pleasure they gave. Perhaps this is because my childish mind loved those plants and gardens for qualities I should now find less important. Were I to look at them with adult eyes, their attractiveness now would be in beauty unrecognized when I was young.

I feel very strongly that a garden is as much an expression of its owner's personality as a painting or any other piece of art he may create. Therefore if his garden is filled with plants he loves and tends with care it will be beautiful, not only to him, but to others who may not share his love of those particular plants. A garden containing the same flowers, planted by a disinterested owner and kept tidy as a dreary duty, somehow lacks the life and lustre of the other, just as a meticulous copy of a masterpiece lacks the spirit of the original.

For enjoyable gardening some knowledge of plants and their requirements is essential, just as it is essential for an artist to understand the materials he uses. But given that basic knowledge, it must be left to each gardener to make his own garden as he wishes it to be. When he fails he will want to know why, and seek to learn how to avoid such failure. The more he learns the more he realizes that a lifetime is not enough to know more than a small proportion of the plants that he could use to make his garden an all-the-year-round delight, to be enjoyed at every season. At this stage some gardeners decide to specialize, and there are societies to encourage and ensnare them; some decide to restrict their horticultural education and consolidate the little learning they already have. Some Philistine few give up, and deny themselves one of the most satisfying outlets creative artistic energy can have.

I

The beginning

 THE SMALL GARDEN OF MY CHILDHOOD HOME IN Belfast, with its damp, dark, acid soil, and its overgrown veronica (hebe) hedge, was not likely to encourage strong, or even weak, horticultural leanings. Apart from carrot tops, orange, apple and grape pips on the window sill, my only other venture was a treasure brought proudly home from the County Down village where we spent our Easter and summer holidays. The donor called it 'Hestia', a name which I have never since been able to track down in any list of common or botanical names. Having tenderly placed my acquisition in the cold black depths of the most promising border available, I never managed to track that down again either, although for at least three years afterwards I searched diligently each spring.

My grandmother had a cottage and a large garden in the seaside village of Killough. It had three bourtrees (elders), a large bush of the ubiquitous veronica, some fuchsia, a climbing pink cabbage rose, a climbing tea rose, quantities of marguerites and attendant blackfly, orange lilies and great clumps of montbretia, long past the best moment for division. There was also a hen run and a vegetable patch. Give or take a cabbage or two, this was the standard content of every garden in the area. I loved it all, even the weeds, which were woven into the fantasies of my childish games.

Every Easter I arrived for the holiday, with my packet of Woolworth's seed, and nursing an ambition which it has taken many long years to outgrow — this summer I would have a blaze of colour . . . a riot of bloom. Usually my uncle had already dug my plot, removed the worst weeds and reduced the soil to a moderate tilth. At the first possible moment I tore open the big outside envelope, gazing with longing at its gaudy picture of an old-world flower garden. Perhaps this would be

15

the year when my wildest dreams and the gaily coloured promise of the seed merchant would be fulfilled. Each year I had a plan, drawn up in an exercise book which was meant for subjects far less fascinating.

The instructions to 'sow thinly' were usually ignored except when I was too generous at the beginning of a row, and the second half was of necessity dealt with sparsely. Such refinements as thinning out and transplanting troubled me not at all, and I never attributed any of my failures to this disregard for time-honoured precept. A depressing anticlimax always followed the first satisfaction of seeing the smooth earth punctuated by sticks carrying the pierced empty packets like little sails. The first few days after planting were always the worst. I would not expect even the most precocious seedling to appear just yet. But towards the end of our stay exciting little green shoots began to show above the ground.

All too soon the Easter holiday ended, and it was frustrating to leave the early fruits of my labours. Then would come the long, long period of waiting. Every week I wrote to my grandmother with anxious queries about the appearance, or non-appearance, survival or demise of my precious seedlings. As the end of June and the beginning of the summer holiday drew near I lay awake at night, savouring the joy of the moment when, with tears of pride, I should view my beautiful flower bed and hear my delighted relatives affirm that undoubtedly mine was the greatest gardening achievement of all time.

Year after year as I surveyed the forlorn reality of my dream, my optimism remained unquenched. Next year would be the year of my success. Each year too, I counted the blessings my weed-ridden plot had provided. Only one sunflower, true . . . but had there ever before been seen such a beauty? Why, it was taller than Uncle Arthur! Nothing but Virginian stock, and it so small and lowly! But at least the wind could not blow that over. What a pity the oranges and yellows of the eschscholzias clashed with the mixed pinks of the clarkia. I was able to close my eyes to such violent disharmony and stand lost in loving wonder and amazement at the crisp pink frills of the clarkia, surely the world's most exquisite flower.

1. The water and peat garden in the third garden after one year

2. *Helichrysum
angustifolium* with
*Ceratostigma
plumbaginoides*

3.*Othonnopsis
cheirifolia* has
attractive glaucous
leaves

One year success did come, and time has never dulled the thrill of it. As I gaze with memory's eye at the blaze of colour of my dream come true I am a child again in Killough, in high summer. I hear the sound of the neighbouring blacksmith's hammer, the hum of bees and clucking of the hens. The sun sparkles on the incoming tide on the other side of the battery wall. The rank smell of a broken branch of bourtree, pushed aside for casting its shadow on my things of beauty, is as unpleasant now as then. Every little packet of Mr. Bee's 'Child's Flower Garden' had excelled in producing its bounty. Virginian stock, mignonette, nemophila, love-in-a-mist, love-lies-bleeding, clarkia, marigolds, gaillardias, larkspur, all clustering round the central towering sunflower. But the crowning triumph of that year was the seemingly infinite variety of the mass of Shirley poppies. Every day brought forth a different, more gorgeous beauty. For the next few years they seeded themselves all over the garden, as did the marigolds, but never again were they so unbelievably beautiful. Nor have any poppies I have seen since brought me such pleasure. The delicate crumpled petals, sometimes white edged with pink, sometimes double, in pink or red, seemed to be intended for dresses for the fairies in whom I so firmly believed until I was nearly thirteen years old.

The cottages along the lower part of Killough Main Street looked across at the little village on the other side of the bay. Then as the street entered the centre of the village it was shadowed by sycamore trees on either side — emerging into the sunlight half a mile further on and becoming once again a single row of cottages looking at the sea. Beyond a stream that ran under the road, houses were described as being 'over the river'. This part of Killough was no promised land overflowing with milk and honey, but gradually dwindled into a stony path leading to the coastguard station. Up here there was a cream painted cottage which every year had a wonderful display of nasturtiums in the narrow border between house and street. It is hard to believe that it is the distance of years that lends enchantment to my recollection of this glowing bed. There may have been caterpillars and snails, and even dandelions among the blooms, but I can see it quite clearly in my mind's eye, and it is still the most magnificent planting of nasturtiums I have seen anywhere, better even than the picture on a seed packet! Certainly no packets of nasturtium seed I have ever sown have done other than produce a depressingly large amount of foliage to flowers, and the stems and underside of the leaves always became encrusted with blackfly before the end of the season, despite my efforts with insecticide. However, the brilliance of the Killough nasturtiums has always remained with me, in spite of my own depressing failures to match their achievement.

Another garden to which I paid yearly homage was the station-master's. Now, I should probably look at both his rockery and rose garden with critical eye, and declare both aesthetically unacceptable, boring and hackneyed, but forty years ago, when schoolfriends and cousins came to stay I took them along to see this wonderful sight.

The rockery, of a type to make alpine gardeners quiver with disdain, was open to the station platform. It never seemed to provide much in the way of the bright colours which were my first love, but I glowed with pride when the visitor murmured in amazement at the range of foliage, for there were cushions and clumps and mats of leaves, glossy, furry, needle thin, or satisfyingly round and fat; bright and dark, olive and sage greens, greys, whites and silvers, and thrilling splashes of red. With the graciousness that befitted my sense of ownership of such a treasure trove (after all I had been coming here every summer since I was born) I allowed those suitably impressed to touch. I could not bear it if they were not as thrilled as I by the feel of those felted silver leaves; by the iron hardness of that mossy emerald cushion which did not even mind being sat upon!

My guests, or perhaps they were my victims, having completed their initiation satisfactorily, were then commanded to climb a high stone wall which was the best, though dangerous, vantage point from which to view the nearest place to Fairyland they would ever see. It was in fact just as I imagined the garden Alice found in Wonderland. Red rambling roses were neatly trained over posts and pillars and chains and pergolas, while at least a dozen standard 'Dorothy Perkins' wept their pink tears into the circular beds of 'Mrs. Sinkins' and godetia at their feet. A magnificent array of red carnations exuberantly lined the path. They smelt of cloves, and often Benny, the porter, called on his way home with a bunch of them for my grandmother. They seemed to me larger and more vivid than any of the flowers she grew, and even the closest inspection never revealed a flaw. The marguerites were never bent by the storm, and large clumps of shasta daisies looked startling against the Virginia creeper which covered the house.

Next, my weary victims were asked to admire the sweetpeas, bigger and better and more sweet smelling. . . . By this time they tended to lose patience and, worse, let their boredom show. So hiding my disappointment that these were not true kindred spirits after all, I would lead them into McCoubrey's field to play hide-and-seek among the haystacks, and flick haws at unsuspecting passers-by. This harmless occupation provided enough excitement to make my friends forget how dull they had found the gardens, and they went home exclaiming what a wonderful time they had had.

I have often wondered what I should think of those gardens in Killough if I could see them now, miraculously preserved as they were all those years ago. It is hard to believe that aphis or mildew would have been permitted to flourish in the station-master's garden . . . that the vivid reds and pinks could possibly have clashed, that the nasturtiums 'over the river' could have hidden their flowers under too vigorous leaves. It is said that it is a mistake to return to places known and loved a long time ago, so I shall always be glad that no return visit has spoilt the vivid pictures I have retained in my memory. I shall always remember the pelargonium in Mrs. Irvine's cottage window as being the most beautiful pot plant I have ever seen. It had great dark maroon flowers with a black blotch in the centre. It never straggled or grew leggy, and was rivalled only by Sarah Jane's enormous salmon-pink and white one, which entirely filled the little window of the house next door. I have tried hard to grow my pelargoniums to that high standard, but somehow they never achieve such opulence. I am sure my memory does not deceive me, and they *were* the truly magnificent specimens I have described.

All my years of effort in gardening have been directed towards creating a garden with the simple charm of those cottage gardens, which seemed always to combine shade and mossy damp with blue skies and sunshine; where the roses were always in bloom and the gooseberries and strawberries always ripe, where the sweetpeas and broad beans stood back-to-back beyond the potato patch; mint and parsley and 'Old Man' provided a foil for bushes of veronica so smothered in purple flowers and butterflies that they seemed to have no leaves at all.

When my efforts with annuals and bedding out have seemed unsatisfying, or when the more sophisticated shrubs and alpines, ordered at such great expense in a moment of weakness at Chelsea, have remained beautiful but unloved, I have often thought of the homely plants of childhood days. They were lovable as well as beautiful, and they looked comfortable in their simple setting. The gardens never looked stiff or contrived. Perhaps the real secret lay in the affection which the owners had for their plants — and of course they only grew plants which they loved.

One of the cruder plantings that charmed me as a child was a clump of lilacs and laburnums overhanging the pavement from the small front garden of a large, terraced corner house near my home. Gardens in Belfast tended to dullness, and therefore the splash of purple and yellow was quite startling among the brick and slate and dusty privet. I looked forward to it each spring, and lingered on my way to and from school to gaze up through the interlacing branches of bloom. I hoped one day to have a like treasury of flowers of my own.

I remembered this when we took possession of our second garden. There they stood, side by side in the February damp and cold. A wispy lilac bush and a spindly laburnum. We watched them anxiously as spring advanced. The lilac did not look very promising and indeed turned out to be a poor specimen of the commonest variety, with small flowerheads of an insipid, washed-out mauve. The laburnum however, kept our hopes alive until the first flower opened. From our reading on the subject we thought it might be *L*. 'Vossii', with the longest racemes of any laburnum. But, if it only had the shorter racemes of *L. anagyroides*, we should be compensated by their abundance. No! It was the biggest disappointment of my gardening life. The flowers were a muddy, dirty pink. I had never heard of a pink laburnum, much less expected to find one growing in my own garden. Frenzied enquiry produced the following facts. . . . Laburnocytisus, a chimera derived from the grafting of *Cytisus purpureus* on to *Laburnum anagyroides*, the scion being accidentally knocked off, leaving a small piece of *C. purpureus* behind. Both stock and the piece of scion sub-sequently grew, the latter within the former, and the resulting growth was therefore the cytisus within the laburnum which formed a layer completely surrounding it. It is called *Laburno-cytisus* × *adamii* after the nurseryman in whose grounds it originated, and is propagated by grafting on seedlings of the common laburnum. The Royal Horticultural Society's *Dictionary* from which I gleaned the above information must have the last word: 'a curious interesting, not particularly beautiful tree . . .'. Certainly its value as a horticultural curiosity never compensated us for its dreary appearance. I had never liked or coveted blue, beige or green roses; nor had I longed for the introduction of a truly pink daffodil. To this list of negatives I added the passionate desire never to see again a mauvish-pink laburnum.

The only comparable disappointment we suffered was over our standard wisteria. It had been with us, planted in several different situations, for eight years before it flowered. Once again we had watched it daily all through that spring. There were five racemes, long and elegant. My husband was the first to discover the secret enclosed in the pale green calyces. He came in from his early morning inspection of the garden and pointed towards the bed on the terrace . . . 'That thing out there, it's white.' 'What thing?' I said, leaving the bacon to burn, as I followed him outside. The first flowers had opened and there was no denying their whiteness. But we both peered and prodded them trying to disprove the evidence. 'No-one has a white wisteria, we can't have one, there isn't such a thing,' I wailed. But people do; we had; there is. Further investigation of gardening encyclopedias and catalogues revealed that our wisteria was the very desirable *W. floribunda* 'Alba'. After we had got over our disappointment at not owning *W. sinensis*, with its cool lavender flowers, we came to appreciate our treasure. Its only fault is that the leaves accompany the flowers, and hide some of their beauty. But it is a most attractive tree and in this standard form easily kept within bounds.

2

Learning by experience and the difficulty of putting away childish things

THERE WAS A LONG GAP IN MY GARDENING CAREER. Although I married during the war, we did not acquire our first house until after my husband's demobilization in 1946. The garden of this, our first real home, was a neglected quarter-acre strip with a few ancient fruit trees. My husband had patience, knowledge, and some skill in gardening matters, as well as a lot of enthusiasm. I had only enthusiasm. As to the first three qualities, patience was my greatest lack. However, we both shared a longing to transform this rather desolate narrow patch into a mass of colour, just like the ones on the seed packets I had so admired as a child.

Martin pruned the roses, mowed the lawn, cut the hedges and produced both vegetables and great clumps of brilliant dahlias and zinnias. During our four summers in that little house his industry and patience were rewarded more fully in each successive season. My spasmodic bursts of enthusiasm produced a few successes and several disasters, from which I learnt some simple, but immensely valuable lessons.

Down one side of the garden a row of Lombardy poplars had been sawn to hedge height. I refused to believe that the ground beneath them was too starved and dry to produce flowers. Hopefully I planted two dozen mixed daffodil bulbs, visualizing gay clumps of dancing yellow flowers belying everyone else's experience. What a miserable thin line of scanty leaves and sparse flowers denied my optimism next spring. I learnt several lessons from that little episode — the un-desirability of Lombardy poplars in the garden; that bulbs for naturalizing tend to be disappointing in their first year and always look better in clumps of a kind, rather than mixed in

23

single file. Unfortunately I did not learn the main lesson —
that the inexperienced gardener does well to heed advice from
experienced gardening friends.

One very hot summer afternoon I decided that the cinder-
covered bare patch under the damson tree would make a
delightful shady lawn. I scraped off the cinders, bought some
grass seed and scattered it on the hard black earth. Martin, on
his return from work shook his head and patiently explained
that even for grass, soil needs to be prepared and levelled, with
a fine tilth on top to take the new little roots. But, even with
that preparation, I had chosen a ridiculous spot: nothing
would grow under the heavily laden damson tree. A few blades
did push through, but there was never enough grass there to
justify mowing, or to deserve the name of lawn.

My sudden vision of a beautiful rockery, aglow with flowers
from spring until autumn, never became a reality either,
although I put tremendous energy into tugging great stones
into place. I wheeled them and pushed them from all over the
garden and from the neighbouring field. I broke my nails and
strained my back, I got very dirty and exhausted — but I only
created an ugly, weed-infested mound of stones in full shade,
which my long-suffering husband eventually removed.

At first we both thought my amaranthus summer a great
success. Every seed in the packet of Love-lies-bleeding must have
germinated. The plants, which filled every available space,
grew enormously. By some strange chance everything favoured
them, and I have never seen such long velvet tassels as those
they produced. But later we realized what an aesthetic calamity
all their depressing drooping maroon panicles were. Not even
the gaudy dahlias could lift the pall of gloom that seemed to
hang over the garden that year.

Next I tried larkspur, clarkia and stocks. The lesson I learnt
that year was that, in gardening, cheerful optimism is not
enough. Soil must be prepared, site carefully chosen, seedlings
painstakingly thinned and watered. Useless to quote my
limited number of past successes, those fortunate plants had
flourished in spite of me and my slap-happy methods. What
about the crooked row of sweetpeas, not double trenched, or

manured — what sparse and straggly blooms they had produced. I decided that gardening was definitely a man's hobby, of which women could enjoy the fruits but not the labour.

I persuaded Martin to saw off an overhanging branch of silver birch, which was shading a spring display of tulips and forget-me-nots. How criminal we felt as day after day the tree's life blood — its fast rising sap — poured down the damaged trunk. Eventually some tar healed the wound and we had both learnt another lesson the hard way, but, looking back, how stupid we were not to have known better!

In an effort to regain some of my horticultural prestige, now so badly tarnished, I mowed the lawn. Ignoring all previous signs of neat trimming, I pushed the mower where I thought it was most needed, sometimes making quite a detour to entrap a sprightly daisy or more flagrant dandelion. Sadly, and as kindly as possible, Martin said that if I felt I really must mow the lawn, which he so much enjoyed doing, he could only wish I would try to do it in straight lines. My indignation knew no bounds and I vowed never again to help in this way. As he liked mowing, he could do it himself from this time forward. . . .

Many years afterwards, when the lawn became my responsibility, and I remonstrated with one of my sons for disregarding the neat pattern of lines made by my previous mowing, I fully understood what a very bad attempt my first effort had been. It was a course of lectures on grass and green keeping that made it clear that a lawn is an area containing thousands of plants (grass) which require light, air, moisture, feeding and weeding just as other plants do. A perfect lawn demands far more care and effort than the average herbaceous border, but it repays its hard-working owner by providing a foil that makes his beautiful flowers look twice as beautiful; and remains green when those flowers have faded.

For the first few years in our second garden Martin tried a number of bedding schemes at the front of the house, with varying success. We both still clung to the view that so long as the beds gave a long period of really bright colour — the choice of plants used to create the display was immaterial.

Red and blue, and white and yellow — the time-honoured bedding plants which were available allowed us a variety of plantings, and it did not matter to us whether the red came from salvias or geraniums, whether the yellow sections were filled with African marigolds or calceolarias. One year we had petunias — a dull summer produced lush foliage and a few flowers. Next year the hot dry season gave us a short burst of flower on the little stunted plants. So we decided a permanent planting of roses was the answer. But first we must fertilize the bed. A local nurseryman promised us some manure — fresh from the abattoir. He must have been amused when Martin arrived with a carful of sacks and buckets to collect it at the end of a very hot August. Of course we should have given it time to rot before we collected it, or added it to the compost heap. But we put it straight on to the bed, right under the sitting-room window.

The car had to be scrubbed with disinfectant to get rid of the smell. The neighbours were good natured about it — although they must have found it as nauseating as we did. This was not the usual farmyard sort of smell, but a peculiar sickly odour accompanied by swarms of flies. Next year we did, however, have excellent roses!

Individual bushes were lovely indeed, but the overall picture was one that left me feeling dissatisfied. We had chosen a random collection of favourites — strong and medium growers, large and small blooms, colours that clashed. We had not yet learnt that every planting should make a picture, with each individual plant or group of plants enhancing its neighbour while showing off its own beauty, for which it had been chosen, and all combining to make a perfect, harmonious whole. To achieve this I no longer plant roses alone, but use under-plantings of bulbs to enliven the ungainly bleakness of the roses in winter, with silver and grey and blue ground cover to make the summer picture satisfying and complete. That belongs to a later chapter, however, and the bed of assorted hybrid tea roses provided many bowls of rich blooms for the house, although we had not then diagnosed its fault as a garden feature.

During our stay in this garden I did little but make sugges-
tions and give unwanted advice from the side lines. Could we
not have a double mock-orange here, a dark red climbing rose
there? At any hint that I might do some weeding or tidying or
sweeping, there was the excuse that the children occupied too
much of my time. At the beginning of our ten-year stay in that
house there were only two children, and the validity of the
excuse was questionable. With three and then four children,
my lack of co-operation over garden chores could not, surely,
be counted as a fault. But, when our fifth child made the family
complete, I was already beginning to take a renewed interest
in gardening, because another move would now be necessary
to a bigger house, and bigger garden.

I nonetheless realized we would be quite sad to leave garden
number two. In spite of the children, several good plants had
managed to survive. They were all well-known, well-tried
shrubs which, with the annual boost of bedding plants, had
achieved our aim of a colourful display, uncomplicated by
correct Latin names and botanical exactitude. Our only two
clematis were 'Jackmanii' and 'Ville de Lyon'; the climbing
roses were such old favourites as 'Emily Gray', 'Étoile
d'Hollande', 'Paul's Scarlet'. As yet our wisteria had not
flowered, but it had been moved from one side of the porch to
the other, and before it had properly recovered from that, we
had decided to train it as a standard. A neighbour had a
beautiful standard wisteria of great age, smothered in lovely
lilac coloured blooms every year. One day ours too might look
like that, so we dug it up and took it with us.

Two plants in particular, which had harsh treatment from
our children, were a rhododendron, and an espalier pear tree.
I had transplanted the former, ball of soil intact as instructed,
early one morning. Three times my two-year-old son arrived
at the kitchen door proudly clutching it by the leaves. Each
time the root ball was diminished a little more, and another
leaf broken. It was finally planted in its corner, where it stayed
flowerless and dejected. The espalier pear was intended to
beautify the fence opposite the kitchen window in spring, and
provide us with fruit in the autumn. With great care and much

reference to our gardening encyclopedia, the site was prepared. Then off we went, with all the children in the car, to the local nursery. My eldest daughter beseeched me to buy one of the dozens of kittens playing around the potting sheds, 'far nicer than a silly old pear tree'. The two older boys chased their younger brother, screaming, round the greenhouses; our younger daughter seemed to grow heavier each minute as we stood and discussed at great length with the nurseryman the best variety to plant. Finally the choice was made, and the plant, carefully wrapped, was placed in the boot. Back we went in triumph, in spite of the fact that two of the children were yelling, and we had been designated heartless for having resisted a particularly appealing tortoiseshell kitten. At last the pear tree was in place, and we retired to the kitchen for a well-earned cup of tea. Fifteen minutes later there was a chorus of: 'Charles has broken the new tree.' He had! The left of its three expensive shoots dangled by a sliver of bark, broken at its base. Of course it had been an accident — he had forgotten about the tree and had ridden too close to it on his tricycle. I tried to placate and comfort my husband by assuring him that in no time at all another branch would grow to replace the one so sadly amputated, but his pessimistic view that the tree was ruined proved to be true. Nothing ever grew on that mutilated left side, and the central stem remained flowerless in sympathy.

There were at that time a number of other horticultural disasters, but of a minor nature, and which did not leave permanent scars on me or the garden.

No one really believed it when I said that I would undertake a full share of the responsibility for the third garden — half an acre this time — but I kept my promise.

3
The real battle begins

 WITH THE MOVE IN 1959 TO OUR THIRD HOUSE, gardening became our all-absorbing hobby and, because this interest was something shared, it brought pleasure more than doubled.

Eleven and a half years were to be spent in the third garden, during which time I worked hard at learning more about horticulture in the various ways described in the following chapters. For nearly six years my husband and I learned and experimented together, but after his death in the summer of 1965 I went on learning alone. The horticultural society was started in the early spring of that year, but I did not attempt the Royal Horticultural Society's general examination until two years later.

Before we could begin to create our new garden there was much to be done. In the dark cold of late autumn, our task seemed daunting. The only assets were a large oak tree, half-way down the lawn, and two well-placed and well-shaped yew trees, making an impressive entrance to the bottom half of the garden which was full of Japanese knotweed. There was a pink-flowered chestnut tree which the children and I counted as a bounty, but which my husband regarded as a threat to the foundations of the house. For the moment, any other possible good features of the garden were shrouded by enormous overgrown laurel hedges, rose briars (end-product of too many untreated suckers in the rose bed), yards of golden privet, holly, sorbus and elder — the whole scene overshadowed by far too many trees. It was like being in an enormous dark room, with green and brown walls and ceiling.

Special permission was needed to have the two great elms at the end of the vegetable plot cut down. A surprisingly poetic Corporation gardener who watched the operation from the other side of the fence said: 'As the first tree fell, I saw the light rush in to fill a place which had been in dark shadow for years past.' Two clear memories remain with me of this incident. The first, the appalling ease with which a man-made instrument of destruction removed those huge trees which it had taken at least sixty years to bring to maturity. The second was when I handed the woodman a cup of tea. He took it with his right hand and saluted his thanks with the other. Horrified, I stared at that left hand from which the electric saw had, some years before, removed two fingers as easily, no doubt, as it had cut the elm branches.

The laurel hedge was nearly 6 feet through — double, staggered planting. We cut it back and took out the front row of bushes. It was a dirty job, and an exhausting one. Secateurs were not enough, many of the branches needed a saw. The immediate result was not impressive. Gaunt, bare trunks allowed in the light, but also an unwanted view of the next-door neighbour's garden. More sun and air and moisture reached the ground elder and bindweed which enmeshed the laurel roots . . . and what a magnificent unwanted crop they produced for the next few years! At last I began to learn the virtue of thoroughness when clearing the ground of perennial weeds.

Such virtue was sorely needed and sorely tried when we tackled the knotweed — *Polygonum cuspidatum*. However deeply we dug, it was always impossible to remove all the penetrating roots. Each tiny piece of root was capable of producing a fine healthy plant within an alarmingly short time. For endless backbreaking hours one summer I painted each little leaf and shoot as it appeared above ground, with systemic weedkiller. That summer was one with more than the usual share of really strong sunshine, which meant that my task, exacting enough in dull weather, became an endurance test, carrying the risk of sunstroke.

The following summer at Chelsea, the representative of the firm responsible for promoting the weedkiller we had used, listened sympathetically to our story of the ominous re-appearance of little polygonum shoots. His advice was to continue digging out each tiny piece of the weed as it appeared. The plant's roots went so deep, that even the weedkiller had only penetrated a part of that depth, while the remnant, healthy and untouched, sent up other shoots from a lower plane. We should eventually weaken the roots by constant removal of the top growth, and digging would, in this instance, be as efficient, and certainly more economical than applications of weedkiller. We followed his advice and conquered our enemy. There are still one or two places where, if unattended, the sleeping monster would raise its ugly head again, so some vigilance is still necessary.

I have always respected the honesty of the salesman, who could so easily have sold us more of his firm's product, but instead chose to tell of the easiest and cheapest way to rid ourselves of this pestilent plant. This honesty I have found in all nurserymen with whom I have had dealings. So often I have wanted to buy a plant, and been refused because the particular growing conditions which I could provide were recognized by the grower to be unsuitable. Another plant would be suggested. When I accepted their advice and planted the alternative they put forward, I have blessed their wisdom. Where I persisted, I have regretted my faulty judgement in not listening to the voice of experience.

While Martin battled on with the moss in the lawn and the suckers on the long-neglected roses, I concentrated on filling the empty spaces. When we had removed overgrown bushes of holly, privet and laurel, we had an empty bed about 90 feet long and 12 feet deep. This we planted with six nepeta, three peonies, three delphiniums, six pyrethrums and six Michaelmas daisies. Sadly we realized that not even the most exuberant growth by these lonely looking inhabitants could possibly turn this piece of ground into a herbaceous border. To buy enough plants to stock it properly would be very costly. I began to beg cuttings and root divisions from my friends — anything to fill the empty spaces. For it had already become obvious to me that just to clear ground was not enough. Ground thus made vacant soon grew an even sturdier crop of weeds, unless some more desirable plant established a prior claim.

Clumps of the most ordinary bearded iris, rudbeckia and solidago were hurriedly planted, while a number of biennials — hollyhocks, sweet williams and Canterbury bells — were sown for next year.

The hollyhocks did not last for long; those that did not blow over, taking their stakes with them, quickly succumbed to rust. The sweet williams were a great stand-by in time of need. Red, pink, salmon and mixed, they filled every gap in the border that year. They also filled four other large beds, but the blaze of colour became rather too dazzling when the nemesias and salvias came into flower. So many warm glowing hues were beautiful, but rather exhausting, and in fact even a little boring. The Canterbury bells were rather a disappointment; obviously I had not been sufficiently ruthless in thinning out, nor sufficiently selective in transplanting only the strongest plants.

The worst mistake I made that year was in edging every bed with *Bellis perennis*. One packet of seed produced more plants than I could use. With a mixture of pride and generosity I distributed the surplus among my friends. I never heard what happened in their gardens, but in ours, after a marvellous display of bloom for many months, they seeded themselves in the lawn, where for the next few years they went on multiplying. Eventually some selective weedkiller containing 2,4-D put an end to their activity, but not before I had learned the truth of the saying that a weed is an otherwise desirable plant in the wrong place.

So many old sayings came alive for me as we toiled and hoped and were sometimes disappointed. None is more apt than the one about patience being a virtue. In an effort to fill the empty spaces, and achieve that highly desirable look of maturity in our borders, we grossly overplanted. Those shrubs and that tree in the narrow border by the front boundary fence looked small and lonely in their first two years — *Daphne mezereum, Malus* 'Neville Copeman', *Deutzia* × *elegantissima, Viburnum carlesii* certainly did not fill the 20-foot stretch. But during the next few seasons I added a *Prunus* 'Amanogawa', sixteen strong-growing floribunda roses, eight *Prunus* × *cistena* 'Crimson Dwarf' aubrieta, clumps of jonquils, daffodils, tulips, crocus, dwarf

4. *Tanacetum densum amanum* on raised island bed

5. *Fuchsia* 'Tom Thumb', 10-12 inches, flowering freely through late summer and autumn

6. *Sedum spectabile* 'Brilliant', a trouble-free perennial attractive in both flower and foliage

7. *Thymus* 'Silver Posy' makes a neat little silver-variegated bush

iris, *Cyclamen neapolitanum*, *Ceratostigma plumbaginoides*, *Geranium dalmaticum*, armeria and *Fritillaria imperialis*. After only seven years I was in trouble. The boundary fence had now gone, and roses spilled out over the pavement, while the overhanging branches of the crab-apple brushed the heads of unwary strangers and our neighbours learned to pass by on the other side. The deutzia's delicate graceful beauty was completely hidden by the strong shoots and dark green foliage of the rose 'Daily Sketch', which also thrust its way through the viburnum; and so many plants overhung the small lawn that it was a nightmare to cut. A little patience, a little restraint in planting, would have produced a more pleasing result and easier maintenance.

Every house to which we have moved has boasted among other undesirable things, at least one broken-down fence. The new oak fence at the back of the herbaceous border looked so stark and so naked that for months all my thoughts and conversation were about plants to cover it. Escallonia, *Garrya elliptica*, *Cotoneaster horizontalis* and climbing roses and honeysuckle were planted. Then came the clematis — seven of them, and *Phygelius capensis*, the everlasting pea 'White Pearl', and *Coronilla emerus* (grown from seed). The honeysuckle smothered one of the roses, and two clematis obliterated the escallonia save for a few despairing little twigs which held their pink blooms aloft, as a drowning man holds up his hands.

Although the total effect was lovely, many good plants were wasted through not having the chance to grow well, so starved and overshadowed were they by their neighbours. There is great art in achieving the richness and perfect satisfaction of a bed well filled with well-grown plants, so massed and grouped as to complement each other without greed or unfair competition.

I did exercise patience in deciding to grow herbaceous plants from seed, only to find some of the subjects I had selected impatient in their bid to colonize larger areas than I could afford them. The worst of these were *Macleaya cordata*, or *Bocconia cordata* as it was then called, *Echinops ritro*, *Achillea ptarmica* 'The Pearl', and *Achillea millefolium* 'Rose Queen'. But

C   33

for a few years, while I became acquainted with, and then acquired, less rapacious perennials, these four filled awkward spaces and gave colour and shape to my borders. I also raised large batches of *Sidalcea* 'Rose Queen', *Physostegia virginica* and *Lychnis chalcedonica*. Now another secret was revealed — the best way to learn about plants is to grow them, and if possible, from seed. Then all the plant's beauty and strength can be appreciated, while its drawbacks and weaknesses are noted too, and the gardener can decide through his own experience whether a plant deserves its place in his garden.

4

Beauty of foliage, form and texture

 FASHIONS ALTER IN GARDENING, AS IN SO MANY OTHER things, and often a capricious change in taste has resulted in many good plants being so neglected that some of them have actually become lost to cultivation. The great surge of interest created by the flower arrangement societies and the attendant search for beauty of form and foliage has greatly enriched our gardens. The combinations of shapes and textures, as well as colours, which made such beautiful arrangements in bowls and vases, began to be used with equal effect and more lasting success in the borders. The desire for unusual material made it exciting to look for rarer varieties which produced variegation, marbling and a wonderful range of colour. Until I became caught up in this obsessive frenzy, I had not really looked at leaves and stems to appreciate their loveliness. I had only seen them as a background and foil for flowers. Then I began to see that if the foliage was attractively massed and placed in the border, with contrasting form and texture and colour — this was satisfying, even when the flowers had faded.

Now, when choosing my plants, those with a short flowering period not complemented by enduring beauty of leaf have to be rejected. When so many plants give value in both flower and foliage over a long period, space cannot be given to inhabitants which do not pay their way. Euphorbias, astrantias, geraniums, hostas, give depth and interest on all counts and add an extra dimension to the garden scene which my once-loved riot of bloom could never do. With hellebores, particularly *H. corsicus* (syn. *H. argutifolius*) and *H. foetidus*, the beauty lasts throughout the year, both being evergreen, but it is not a static beauty. At one stage the flower-laden shoots of *H. corsicus* fall outwards to show the fresh strong shoots springing up in the centre. The foliage of *H. foetidus* is, I think, the loveliest of all the hellebores, elegantly fingered and dark green, it deserves a place in the garden in August, as much as in March, when the panicles of small, red-tipped light green cups are held high above the leaves.

Perhaps the most intriguing variations of form and texture are to be found in grey and silver plants. Many of these look respectable all through the winter months, and help to soften and lighten the sometimes rather sombre picture made by stark deciduous trees and evergreens. *Helichrysum angustifolium*, *Leucanthemum hosmariense*, the santolinas, *Senecio greyi*, are the ones that in my garden retain their beauty, and contribute in this way. Not only is there a wonderful range of leaf shapes — filigree, feathered, lacy, sculptured, round and needle thin, but the shades of grey, silver, white and glacial green add lustre to the border at all times of the year. Although some gardeners emulate the white and silver garden of Sissinghurst Castle, I agree with those who aver that such plantings need the highlights that splashes of colour can provide. Often, silver plants can tone down too harsh contrasts, and provide a unifying link between otherwise unrelated groups.

The newly formed Flower Arranging Club which I had joined was a great source of cuttings. At first the main attraction was the inspiration to arrange flowers and so satisfy a creative urge which I had previously thought could only be satisfied by painting pictures. My artistic yearnings had hitherto remained unfulfilled, because my practical nature could not bear to fill the house with quantities of amateurish paintings. I had no confidence that my work would be anything but third rate, or that it would do other than gather dust in the attics, or clutter the walls of my house. Flower arrangements would only last a short time, and never long enough to be an embarrassment. We had demonstrations of this art by experts, and we had classes for novices like myself. I went along to my first class with a dozen irises and a very large bowl, hoping that by some magic I would be taught how to make a beautiful arrangement with these. How the instructors laughed! For such a large bowl armfuls of flowers would be needed. They found me a smaller container and some foliage and did their best.

Soon my interest moved from the demonstrator's skill to the fantastic variety of foliage and flowers they used — mostly from their own gardens. Sometimes we were given pieces of a much admired plant, or a precious piece would be raffled to be borne home with pride, followed by the envious eyes of fellow members.

I now have a collection of bergenias, but my very first bergenia, the common *B. cordifolia*, came from a friend's garden after I had attended my first Flower Club meeting, and admired the russet tinted, leathery leaves used at the base of an arrangement. I remembered where I had seen it growing quite near my home. My friend looked rather bewildered when I came panting to her door in the foggy November dusk.

'Please, you have a plant among the weeds at the bottom of the garden, and I won't spoil anything if you'll let me take a bit, because I've just seen it used at the Flower Club — and it's beautiful, and I know just where to get it.' 'You are very welcome to have as much as you like — I'll come down the garden with you, I didn't know we had any good plants there — my husband will be pleased.' But she was disappointed at my choice — she knew 'Elephants' Ears' well, but it had not yet come fully into fashion. As with so many of the foliage plants, now much sought after for their beauty of form and texture, it was the flower arranging movement that was largely responsible for making us look and really see the fine qualities of this formerly despised plant.

After a few years, I, too, had a flower arranger's garden — lovely and unusual shrubs and herbaceous plants, with a tremendous variety of form, colour and texture of leaves and flowers. But having grown them I was loth to cut them, I enjoyed them so much more in the garden than in the house, where their lives were shortened.

So, I became a 'lapsed' flower arranger and an even more dedicated gardener than before.

It was the Flower Club instruction in design that made me alert to design in groupings for the borders. All the precepts laid down by the skilled and artistic demonstrators brought the satisfaction of success when followed in the garden. I learned that if the design of my garden was bad, if it had a poor 'skeleton', no amount of planting and camouflage would compensate or disguise this fact. The best time of year for discovering what is wrong with one's garden is mid-winter, when all the floral frills and furbelows of summer have gone. It is then that perfect balance and good design show up most clearly. This is when knowledge of how to correct poor design can most effectively be gained. It is like making a really accurate pencil drawing before applying the colour. I used to go up to the second floor, and spend hours just looking, noting what displeased or dissatisfied me — a bare fence needing evergreen cover, or the need for a tall slim conifer to add all-the-year-round height to a bed curiously flattened, when its important herbaceous focal point had withered. I could see where golden foliaged heathers, or variegated vincas could lighten whole areas, and bring the illusion of sunlight to an otherwise gloomy corner. Those straight-edged borders that looked quite good in midsummer when seen from ground level, looked gauche and inelegant from my high vantage point. The same guides to proportion of height and width apply to flower beds as to any flower arrangement. We do the plants we love a great injustice if we ignore the laws of proportion, and group them awkwardly in beds of the wrong shape and size.

Simplicity, lack of fussiness, natural flow from one group of plants to another in a carefully planned symmetry that yet appears uncontrived, that seems to have happened effortlessly — these are as much the hallmarks of good garden planting as of good flower arrangements.

The genus *Hosta*, more than any other, owes its present well-deserved popularity to the flower arranging movement. Any who saw the wonderful exhibit of hostas staged by the Royal Horticultural Society at Chelsea a few years ago could not be other than impressed by its undoubted and varied elegance of leaf, colour and variegation. Descriptions of any hosta usually end with such a phrase as 'the rather insignificant lily flowers are of little importance'. I have always admired their beautiful simplicity and would not so readily dismiss them.

One negative result of my dalliance with flower arranging

was the development of a hearty dislike of competition. The first reason for this was, I think, caused by the detrimental effect of the competitive spirit on the arrangers themselves. Instead of enjoying their flowers, they often came to regard them as a mere tool for floral one-upmanship. Then there were the more obvious dangers of the judge downpointing an arrangement because of personal preference for other colour schemes or designs, when possibly the rejected entry was an honest piece of self-expression created by flowers grown and cherished by the arranger, while the winning entry, although slick and eye-catching, had cost its experienced creator very little in artistic effort and loving thought. Obviously paintings, sculptures, flower arrangements entered for competitions, must all reach a certain standard. But after that standard has been reached, the top award can only be made by the arbitrary decision of the adjudicator, quite naturally influenced by her own likes and dislikes. I very much favour the non-competitive exhibitions and displays now more in vogue. I strongly believe that each person's garden should be seen and appreciated as its owner's individual achievement in terms of artistry and love, knowledge and skill. Comparisons are odious — and in this case it seems to me quite abhorrent to reduce a garden's merits to its relative triumph or failure beside other gardens. Obviously we all like certain types of gardens more than others; no two of us like exactly the same sort of garden. Let us therefore be content to differ, but not be so discourteous, nor so presumptuous as to make judgements, and give or withhold prizes.

5

The academic approach

 IN SPITE OF ALL MY READING, I FELT RATHER AS IF I had cheated by not beginning at the beginning. There is a stolid, humourless streak in me that demands that I begin any task, be it learning Italian, reading a book, or learning about gardening, at the beginning and then plod determinedly through to the end. Sometimes the end is unattainable, or my determination falters long before it is in sight. But even to reach the half-way mark without having trodden firmly on every preceding rung, leaves me feeling dissatisfied and slightly guilty.

It was with great delight, therefore, that I accepted an invitation to join a beginners' gardening class at Leamington Further College of Education. The course was organized for members of the Women's Institute, and I qualified only by being a beginner. Each afternoon gave time to both practical work as well as theory. First, we were taught the correct way to handle a spade. Having chosen the right spade for each individual's size and strength, we went out on to the trial garden and were shown how to dig, trench and double trench. Then followed instruction in the use of the hoe, rake and fork. We learnt about making a compost heap and the elements needed for balanced growth. We were told which natural and which artificial fertilizers supplied these. It was like learning a new language. After being taught about the lawn, we thinned and transplanted seedlings and took cuttings. There were complete sessions on plant identification. It was great fun, and I felt I was really beginning to be a gardener. Sometimes our teacher gave us a few treasures to take home. One of these was *Morina longifolia*. None of us had ever seen the plant before, but since then I have read several articles commending it as a very desirable plant. It has jagged, thistle-like leaves forming a central crown from which rise leafy spikes 2 feet long, bearing crowded whorls of white tubular flowers. These flowers gradually become a delicate pink and finally crimson.

These classes took place over eight years ago, and apart from my increased virtuosity with spade, fork and fertilizer, I still have several cherished plants, propagated afresh each year from divisions of the original little pieces carried home with great care from the college. *Lychnis flos-jovis* has given me great pleasure. It is an old-fashioned plant, rose-pink, about 1 foot high, and it has shared a sunny position with laced pinks and *Euryops acraeus* (syn. *E. evansii*). It dislikes winter wet, but I have always managed to save it by putting granite chippings round its collar.

Two other plants were *Helxine solierolii* 'Aurea', and 'Variegata' — gold and silver Mind-your-own-business. The two pieces I was given were very tiny — but each succeeding year I divided them and threw lots of last year's growth away. I content myself with twenty 3-inch pots of each, and another ten of each to give to friends. I also keep about a dozen pots of the plain green to act as foil to the lighter colours. They are so easy to grow and yet are so seldom seen. They make a bright and pretty edging to tidy up the heterogenous collection of pelargoniums, fuchsias and echeverias which cram my little conservatory. The gold and silver grow as well and as strongly as the green, and all three have a crisp freshness which always delights — but I do keep them confined to their pots, for like even the most charming children, when allowed too much license, they become unmannerly and a nuisance.

Each week I returned home with copious notes and a lot of good advice for my husband, who with great trust and good nature followed my instructions on making compost heaps, managing lawns and taking cuttings. Unfortunately there were a few times when I had only grasped half the story, but innocently passed it off as the whole truth. One such occasion was when I assured Martin that sulphate of ammonia would help the grass grow lush and green and, by increasing the soil's acidity, would discourage coarse grass, clover and worms. But I got my quantities wrong, telling him to apply 2 ounces per square yard instead of $\frac{1}{2}$ an ounce. Neither did I remember that sulphate of ammonia should only be applied when rain is expected shortly afterwards, otherwise it must be copiously watered in. A warm dry spell followed that evening's work of mixing the straight fertilizer with sand as a spreader and scattering it as evenly as possible at the rate just mentioned. Martin's misgivings were well founded but, with great forbearance, his only comment on the awful brown scorched patches was that next time I must be quite certain of my facts.

Many of the things I learnt were retailed accurately, and we had tremendous fun in putting them into practice. One spring we spent hours on the neighbouring common cutting young bracken shoots as a mulch for our newly planted azaleas. Later in the year we collected barrow loads of dry bracken to protect some tender plants from the rigorous winter that was forecast. Martin was quite undeterred by the hazards of cutting young nettles to help our compost heap heat up quickly, when we were told of this weed's hitherto unknown usefulness. The compost heap became quite an obsession with us, and we threw up our hands in equal horror at orange peel in the dustbin, or milk bottle tops in the compost bucket.

The soil of our third garden was the usual worn-out soil of an old town garden, sadly lacking not only humus, but various essential major and trace elements necessary for good plant growth. The most desirable remedy, farmyard manure, was expensive and not easily obtainable. By the small supplement scraped off the roads — to my children's great embarrassment — I could only hope to profit a very limited area. However, I carried a plastic sack and a shovel in the boot of my car and, in spite of being assured that I looked eccentric, that everyone was staring at me and that the smell was unendurable, I managed to collect a small amount of manure for specially deserving plants.

The compost heap was intended to supply a substitute for farmyard manure and, in order to build a satisfactory one, coarse material or rows of bricks are needed at the bottom of the heap to allow the free passage of air underneath. The ideal heap should not be more than 5 feet square, or be built higher than 4 feet. All the annual weeds, dead heads, stalks and foliage from the border, grass mowings (in thin layers), dead leaves and vegetable waste from the kitchen are ingredients for the pile. They should be spread on the heap in 3- to 4-inch layers, with a sprinkling of soil on the surface of each layer. A proprietary activator can then be added to the soil layer surface, or lime and sulphate of ammonia to alternate layers. Better still — and I can do this now that I live in the country and keep hens — add a layer of poultry manure as an activator. The heap should be watered regularly and thoroughly. Advice varies on whether to turn, or not to turn, the heap over at intervals. Personally we found it advantageous to turn it once, when half made. Woody material should be well chopped and broken, or omitted altogether. No diseased material should be used.

We found that a heap started in spring could be used by midsummer as a top dressing or mulch, and the midsummer heap would be ready by autumn. Rotting down during the winter months was slow, but we usually had some autumn-started compost ready during spring to early summer.

However, all this was not sufficient, and we had to supplement it with balanced fertilizer mixes to supply further nourishment to the hungry soil. At one stage I did quite a lot of damage by experimenting with 'straight' fertilizers, an area where a little knowledge is a very dangerous thing. By applying these unwisely and without full knowledge of one's soil, imbalances and further deficiencies can be caused. One very welcome Christmas present was a simple soil-testing kit, which told not only the pH, or lime content of the soil, but the nitrogen, phosphate and potash level.

We aimed at having a pH of 6.5, which is slightly acid, and suits a wide variety of plants. At pH 6.5 the availability of nitrate nitrogens, phosphates, potassium and magnesium is at its highest level, organic matter rots easily, as it will not do in an over-acid soil, and there is a reasonable availability of the trace elements necessary for healthy plant growth.

Poor soil structure and aeration can result in a nutrient deficiency in plants lacking a healthy root system. The plant's efficiency depends on its root system, and roots need oxygen to live. For free movement of oxygen in the soil it must be well drained. Good drainage depends on good soil structure. Where a particular nutrient is in short supply, poor rooting may be sufficient to cause a deficiency in the plant.

We also became quite fanatical about the advantage of mulching. This enthusiasm was triggered off by a visit to a friend's garden which was kept weed-free and beautifully tidy by a 3-inch layer of spent hops. He told us where to obtain this mulching material, which would only cost us the price of the transport. It was May, and the ground had warmed up after a mild wet spring, so Martin lost no time in ordering a load (there is of course no food value in the spent hops themselves: so-called hop manure contains added nutrients). The wet, smelly stuff had to be dumped in the yard in front of the garage, blocking access completely. Against instructions, we started to move it immediately, hoping to weaken the sickly odour of stale beer, and render it less offensive to our family and neighbours. Martin shovelled it into one barrow and brought it to me and, while I carefully placed it round the plants, he filled the second barrow. It was a backbreaking task for both of us, but the result was most pleasing and rendered the labour of weeding almost negligible that summer. We had of course weeded and broken up the soil in the beds very carefully before putting on the mulch.

There were two minor snags. The birds loved scratching around in the spent hops and thus tended to cover up small plants, and the lawn edges. Vigilance in examining the beds daily, and returning the mulch to its proper place in the parts of the garden where the birds wreaked this havoc, kept everything under control. Extra care had to be taken with pinks, silver plants and delphiniums, which did not appreciate moisture round their collars. We placed limestone chippings round the pinks, and coarse sand round the other plants, and this was sufficient to keep them happy and healthy.

Although it is recommended that grass mowings be composted before being used as a mulch, I have found them useful in a 3- to 4-inch layer round shrubs, and put on without first

44

composting. They have been particularly successful in a cool moist summer when the grass is growing fast and when annual meadow-grass in seed is absent. They quickly rot down and smother the weeds which would otherwise multiply rapidly, and may also help condition the soil. The great danger of mulching with uncomposted material is that there will be nitrogen theft from the soil to help decomposition of the mulch, thus impoverishing the soil instead of enriching it. But with the addition of sulphate of ammonia I have even used sawdust effectively.

After the first course finished, I attended an amateur gardening class at the local technical college. The students were more mixed in age, intellect and occupation than any group I have ever seen. I was fascinated that the love of gardening could unite such a motley collection. There was one lady in her late seventies who looked unbelievably fragile, but who turned up each week, despite adverse weather; who never dozed, and was as eager as any to collect her full quota of the seedlings and cuttings so generously offered by the lecturers. There were also young married couples, embarking nervously on their first garden, seasoned chrysanthemum or vegetable growers, typists and teachers, housewives and bus conductors.

The lecturers in charge of the course were lively and imaginative in the way they shared their incredible store of knowledge with us. We had talks and demonstrations, films and slides, leaflets and printed notes on the lectures. Our questions were answered patiently and at the beginning of each session there was a display of plants and shrubs labelled with both common and botanical names, origin, and habit of growth. These were examined and handled while our teacher went on to tell us how to propagate each one, compared one species with another and listed the virtues of the newest cultivars. I still have three *Paeonia delavayi* grown from seed given at one of these classes, and a flourishing little *Thujopsis dolabrata* which has developed from a minute cutting from a small branch of the shrub divided among at least ten students after a talk on conifers.

So absorbing did I find their approach, that next year I joined the day-release class of Parks and Garden students studying for the Royal Horticultural Society's general examination in horticulture. The young men looked surprised to see such a very mature student join them, the only other female being a girl in her teens, but they were kind and friendly, and soon accepted me. The studies involved one whole day per week, and meant for me a complicated system of baby-sitters and advance preparation of meals.

The first half of the morning was taken up with horticultural botany, which I enjoyed tremendously. The rest of the morning was given to another part of the syllabus — vegetables, fruit, flowers or greenhouse management. In the afternoon we had practical work, and an hour's training in plant recognition. In the evening the two-hour lecture was on grass and green-keeping, and we were joined by student groundsmen from various parts of the county. I had never expected to know how to lay drains on a football pitch, nor hoped to memorize the correct proportions of a bowling green, nor did I think I should ever have occasion to use the information I acquired about gang mowers. But it was worth learning about things irrelevant to home gardening in order to learn also about different types of grass and their uses, fertilizers, and recognition and treatment of lawn weeds and diseases.

My children were amused to see me labouring over my homework. I had no time to watch television. My evenings were spent poring over my books. Sometimes I was weary during lectures and began to nod off, but my neighbour obligingly plied me with peppermints when excessive fidgeting told tales of my struggle to stay awake!

During the weeks before the examination I had misgivings about my ability to remember all the facts and marshal them in a form which would convince the examiners of my worthiness to receive a pass mark. It seemed obvious that the reason there were no other middle-aged women doing the examination was that I was the only one foolish enough not to realize the limitations that age imposed upon mental agility. When the great day arrived, even the invigilator was rather surprised to see me!

But to my great relief the questions were not beyond me — I wrote furiously non-stop up to the end of the time allotted for each paper, and in due course received the happy news that I had passed with distinction.

Far from making me have a false sense of achievement — all this instruction made me realize how vast the subject of horticulture, and how relatively small the share of wisdom, I had gained. But now, having mounted the first few steps in this way, I felt the confidence to go on climbing.

Previously I had regarded people who used Latin names for plants as horticultural snobs and pedants. The classes at the technical college provided an introduction to the fascinating study of nomenclature and showed how important the Latin names were. I found that whereas the so-called common names were often local in application, Latin naming was international. True, botanists have a nasty habit of changing names just when one has mastered a particularly difficult one, but often their reasons for so doing uncovered an intriguing period of the plant's history. The library contained several books which explained how the names were formed, and gave their meanings. This led to further reading about the plant collectors after whom some plants were named, and soon I was brushing up my history so as to fit these exciting stories into their correct period. So many plants formerly taken for granted were regarded in a new light when I read of the dangers and hardships endured by these brave men in order to introduce them to this country.

The history of gardens and gardening was one more part of the ever-expanding field of pleasurable study to which the gardening lectures had opened the gate.

6

Shows, societies
and other sources of information

 BECAUSE MY REAL INTEREST IN GARDENING DID NOT begin until I was nearly forty, I was afraid that I had too short a time in which to learn enough to make gardening the satisfying occupation it should be. Trial and error were leading so slowly to increased knowledge. Besides, a negative approach to a creative pastime frustrates real enjoyment. The painful lessons of experience are certainly necessary, but should be assimilated with the help of some positive aids.

Apart from picking the brains of gardening friends and taking to heart their words of advice, there were at least half a dozen other sources of knowledge which I tapped during the next few years. First there were the regular gardening articles in the Sunday papers and Saturday editions of two dailies. Martin used to go to his office each Saturday morning, and the most important thing from my point of view was that he returned with the *Financial Times* whose gardening column was always tremendously interesting and set me off on a search for many a good plant. One week, the writer of one of the Sunday columns advised his readers to make a collection of some of the nurserymen's catalogues. These, he assured us, would form an excellent and inexpensive nucleus of a gardener's library. After all, the man who has grown good plants and seeks to sell them, wishes to inform his customers on the best choice of plant for their local growing conditions. A customer educated in this respect is much more likely to be a satisfied one. Immediately I wrote off to the firm recommended, carefully noting which ones required a nominal sum to cover cost and postage. We spent many happy and profitable hours poring over this catalogue library. Over the years it has grown, and never fails as a source of information and inspiration. I know of many other gardeners who keep a pile of these useful books by their bedsides. All are agreed what a wonderful service the nurserymen thus provide at a ridiculously low cost.

Having learnt all we could from the description of a particular plant in one of these books, sometimes with accompanying illustration, it was always a thrill actually to see it either at a show or in a garden. Every weekend in the summer, we used to go off to one of the many gardens open to the public in aid of charity. As the children got older, they too enjoyed these outings. Very often the head gardener or the owner-gardener would be there to talk about his plants, and to bask in the interest and admiration of visitors.

It was on such a visit that we were introduced to the rose 'Guinée'. Although this particular open day was too early for us to see the rose in bloom, we were entranced by the gardener's poetic description of its velvety texture and glorious scent. He was so obviously a very practical man, who worked hard with his small staff to keep these gardens lovely. Such a man would not easily be led into a rapturous description, full of superlatives. Everything he told us about it was true, and we have loved it for its form, its colour, its texture and its perfume, but above all for the picture it recalls of the man's face, homely and unassuming, alight with pleasure, as he tried with an unexpectedly poetic turn of phrase to make us appreciate the qualities of his favourite rose.

A visit to Rowallane, County Down, was made on a day when the gardens were not officially open to the public. Martin managed to persuade Mr. Hanvey, the head gardener, to allow us in, promising to keep his eye on me, in response to the jocular comment that women were not to be trusted to restrain their greedy fingers from taking illicit cuttings! As a reward for being good, I was given two hips of *Rosa moyesii*. These I carefully ripened and planted. By the next sad summer, when Martin died suddenly, the pots still showed no signs of life. But the following spring, eighteen months after sowing, I had fifteen little seedling rose trees. I was very touched at this living memento of our happy visit to Northern Ireland. I kept three, and they are now large bushes. The young foliage is delicate and fern-like, and I think this rose would be worth growing for the leaves alone. The short-lived single red flowers are the second joy it brings. Last of all come the enormous flagon-shaped brilliantly coloured hips, for which I first admired it.

Our first visit to Chelsea Flower Show was one of the most wonderful outings we ever had together. It stands high in my memory as an event equally exciting as other highlights, such as our first visit to the Bernese Oberland; seeing the 'Fall' splendour in Vermont; our first swim on Wakiki beach. These last three were spectacular in their own particular ways, but not so breathtaking nor so beautiful as that trip to Chelsea. We realized at the start of our gruelling day that we could not hope to see and enjoy everything there, so on arrival we sat down quietly with a cool drink and our catalogue, and decided which were to be our priorities. Everything seemed so much better than we had expected — and we had been expecting a lot. The water gardens, of which we had read so much, ex-ceeded all the descriptions. Then there were the shrubs, the roses, the peonies, the herbaceous plants, the alpines — and of course Miss Havergal's tantalizing strawberries. No weary desert traveller could feel more frustrated when, parched with thirst, he cannot reach the oasis, than the tired Chelsea devotee faced with Waterperry's forbidden fruit.

The previous year I had bought Martin some shrubs chosen from the first catalogue of my collection, that of a famous North of Ireland nursery. This purchase represented our first step towards careful selection of the best variety of plant, chosen to give full garden value. Although the order had not been a large one, I had had two queries to make about my choice, and the resulting correspondence with the nurseryman had impressed us greatly, because of the time and trouble he took in explanation and advice. The first question was prompted by an article in the *Sunday Times* which suggested that *Viburnum carlesii* was better when grown on its own roots, as grafted specimens tended to sucker. This nursery was the one mentioned as having such plants. But I was advised by the grower that they were very small plants, which would take a long time to establish, and that the grafted ones which they supplied were well-grown shrubs which should give no trouble. I can honestly say that the one they sent is the finest *Viburnum carlesii* I have ever seen, beautifully shaped, and covered in its sweet-scented bloom every year. I have never regretted taking his other excellent piece of advice and choosing *Malus* 'Neville Copeman' as a specimen ornamental crab, instead of 'John Downie'. In winter it is an elegant shape, in spring the red leaves and pink blossom are a delight, and in autumn, and well into winter the large orange-red fruit gives a striking display of colour. Although I am always loth to pick them, they make delicious ruby-red apple jelly.

So it was tremendously exciting to find our way first of all to his stand, and admire examples of the very plants we had chosen, so much more mature than ours, but assuring us that the promises of the catalogue descriptions would be fulfilled, as indeed they have been.

Indeed the next year, on our second visit, Mr. Slinger could not have been more helpful or attentive had our anxious questions concerned several acres of plants purchased from him, instead of our two little escallonias cut to the ground by the severe winter, and still, at the end of May, looking unmistakably dead. He told us not to give up hope, to cut them back fairly hard, to keep them watered and, above all, to have patience. He was right. In July there appeared on their dead looking twigs some tiny green buds — so tiny that we had to lie full length on the lawn to see them properly. We felt as joyful as the woman in the Bible who found the coin which was lost, but when we called to our children to rejoice with us they were merely a little puzzled by their parents' peculiar behaviour. Those two escallonias have flourished ever since. I am never quite sure which is my favourite, 'Apple Blossom' or 'Donard Radiance', the flowers of both are so profuse, and each individual bloom so exquisite at a time when not many flowering shrubs, save roses, are in bloom. I have given away a great many cuttings of both, as this shrub strikes easily.

This readiness to discuss the plants on show with potential customers is the very best kind of good salesmanship. There is never any question of presuming on the ignorance of the customer in order to make a sale, however unsuitable the purchase to his growing conditions. Such a policy is short-sighted, whatever the article being sold, but how seldom salesmen of other wares exercise the tact, patience and foresight of nurserymen.

So often, the second visit to the scene of a previous pleasure proves almost unbearably disappointing. I have never found this with Chelsea Flower Show. However unfriendly the weather, or unpropitious the season, however late the train or however great the pressure of the crowds, there is always the same mounting excitement and sheer joy in just being there, with so much beauty to delight us.

The shows held in the Royal Horticultural Society's halls at Vincent Square are another source of perfect enjoyment. I know of nothing to compare with the exhilaration that follows the moment of unbelief on entering the New Hall on a cold, wet February day, when the first show of the year fills it with the scent of hamamelis, mahonia and viburnum. As one examines the huge branches of winter flowering shrubs, cut with such lavish hands for the competitions, one discovers that there are many more heavily perfumed blooms than these three. All are in such wonderful condition that one needs to read the schedule once again to be reassured that in our much maligned British winter, these were indeed grown outside 'without protection'. I always linger over that delightful moment of indecision — to look first at the magnificent array provided by the competitive classes, or to spend the first hour browsing round the rock garden stands showing a bewildering number of tiny bulbs and early alpines, all in full bloom and fresh perfection. Then, too, there are the stands showing the winter and spring flowering shrubs grown in carefully simulated woodland gardens and shrub borders. I have never been strong enough to attend one of these shows without ordering yet more plants for my already over-crowded garden, and spending the rest of the week justifying my extravagance as necessity; but who could resist, when the nurserymen, without the thronging crowds of Chelsea, have more time to answer all the questions, and to give advice on which of their plants would or would not grow in each enquirer's garden. Their courtesy, like their patience and their knowledge, seems inexhaustible.

After lunch, and time spent reading through the notes and catalogues already collected, back into the hall for another look round before going upstairs to the lecture. Then a cup of tea, and a short walk round the corner to the Old Hall to visit the Lindley Library. After a quiet half hour spent looking up references to a plant that has caught my eye, it is time to catch my train. The journey back to Coventry is long enough to enable me to finish reading the newly acquired horticultural literature. These outings made, either by choice or necessity, alone, were always completely satisfying. Although there was no one with whom to share each reaction of wonder, admiration or appreciation, one look around sufficed to confirm that these emotions were being felt by the other visitors to the stands. Indeed, unless I could have had Martin as my companion, it was better to be alone than risk the jarring note of an unsympathetic friend who did not feel as I did about the magic quality of the shows. Once my elder daughter, a nurse at a London hospital, came with me, and my pleasure in all I saw was increased by her enjoyment, so like my own, and nothing was spoilt. She had considered her precious off-duty well spent, and this was proof enough of her genuine appreciation.

The first time I saw *Crocus chrysanthus* was at a show at the Royal Horticultural Society's halls in Vincent Square. There were so many varieties from which to choose, and each was so beautiful, that I prowled and pondered for at least an hour before deciding on 'Blue Pearl' and 'Cream Beauty'. Although I have since planted many others, all lovely, these still remain my favourites. There always seems to be an incredible pathos about the clumps of delicately coloured little flowers as they open wide in the wintry sunshine, and remain unblemished by the biting weather. They seem almost like innocent children, preserved from harm by their very beauty and purity and the naïveté which makes them play in very flimsy clothing, unscathed, when everyone else is muffled against the treacherous winds of February and March.

Another time I spent the whole morning at a stand devoted

entirely to snowdrops. This was a revelation, as up till then snowdrops had been distinguished for me by being single or double, large or small. This was a superb exhibit, moss and grass and a few dead leaves covered the ground from which these beauties grew, highlighted here and there by a few aconites. At first it was just the artistry that attracted me. Then I studied the nearby display of photographs and botanical drawings. There was more there than could be learnt in an hour, or even two. As I turned back to the flowers I felt very humble when I realized how many plant collectors and botanists, how much learning and research, had combined to make this exhibit possible. It inspired in me the same mixture of delight and awe and gratitude as a great painting in an art lover or an exquisite symphony in a musician. On my visit to the library that afternoon, I borrowed Mr. Bowles's book *Snowflakes and Snowdrops*. This confirmed my realization that I had not even begun to learn about plants. Although I could only afford a modest order, 'Sarah Arnott', 'Atkinsii', *viridapicis*, and *elwesii* were ordered 'in the green' and they have increased each year and been a source of great joy.

Talking of snowflakes reminds me of the great disappointment the year after planting *Leucojum vernum*. Out of six bulbs, only three appeared. I was quite distressed, and blamed the slugs. But next year all six came up, and have flowered and increased each year since. Apparently this quite often happens, and they should be bought and planted 'in the green' like snowdrops. I have only recently seen them offered for sale thus, with the explanation that in the same way as snowdrops, they resent an interruption of their growth cycle. When left out of the ground for too long the bulbs are very inclined to develop a fungus attack.

Although at first acquaintance a cursory glance might deceive one into thinking leucojums and snowdrops very much alike, the differences are quite distinctive. The summer snow-flake, *Leucojum aestivum*, is lovely with its 18-inch arching stems, but *L. vernum* is for me the most exciting of the genus, its large, bell-shaped flowers tipped with green, defying the worst February weather.

It was after the second show of the year, at the end of February that my most successful venture came to be. I was preparing lunch for my family, and dinner for some guests the same evening. In the mingling steam of boiling potatoes and washing up I thought of the Royal Horticultural Society's halls the day before; so many beautiful plants, so many knowledgeable people. How was I ever going to learn even a fraction of what they knew? The lecture had been excellent, the lecturer famous. No one like that ever came to Coventry . . . supposing there were a horticultural society . . . perhaps I could start one!

I dealt with the potatoes and rang up Martin.

'Do you think I could start a horticultural society here in Coventry so that we could have lectures like they do at the R.H.S.?' Martin, who always remained quite calm during my sudden bursts of enthusiasm, was cautious but encouraging. So I rang the three women who were coming to the dinner party. 'If I start a horticultural society for women, so that we can have first-class lecturers, and really learn about plants, will you join? Think about it and tell me tonight.' They were surprised, but acquiescent.

That afternoon I started making plans for a society, which would have about sixty members, no competition and a subscription of 25 shillings a year. I telephone several local halls to find out possible bookings, fees and so on, explaining that the whole affair was still only a hypothesis. Then I wrote to several nurserymen and to Mrs. Margery Fish, outlining my idea, and asking: 'If I start this society, will you come and speak, and how much will you charge?'

Another letter went off to the Royal Horticultural Society asking for advice and instruction on the formation of a horticultural society, and letters to three of the popular gardening magazines. Only after all these had been posted did I get back to preparations for the evening's entertaining. My guests', like my husband's, reaction to my detailed account of all this activity, was a blend of approval, scepticism and resignation. 'What a good idea — if it works; it probably won't, but she's going to do it whatever we say.'

7

The Women's Horticultural Society, Coventry

 I WASTED NO TIME, AND SPENT MOST OF THE NEXT day telephoning my friends to ask them — and any other interested people — to come to my house for coffee two weeks later, when I would tell them all about the proposed society. Meanwhile I received replies with advice and offers of help from the Royal Horticultural Society, the local technical college, and the Parks and Gardens director. Mrs. Fish kindly wrote and wished me well and agreed to come and give a talk if required, in October.

When the day of the coffee morning came, I had no idea how many people to expect, but I had all my facts assembled and hoped to persuade them to dignify this new venture with the name of 'Horticultural Society' rather than 'Garden Club'. I was determined too that we should be 'women' and not 'ladies'!

Forty guests arrived for coffee and listened attentively to what I had to say — they agreed to all proposals about naming the society, that it should be affiliated to the Royal Horticultural Society, be non-competitive, aim high and invite top-ranking speakers, and have a sales table for selling members' surplus seedlings and cuttings cheaply. The day for meeting was fixed for the second Wednesday afternoon of each month (except August) beginning in April. Volunteers made up the steering committee, with myself as chairman. We were extremely fortunate in having among these volunteers a very capable treasurer, who actually wanted to be treasurer, and a perfect secretary who had come armed with a portable typewriter, as she had intended to offer her services in this capacity. She felt it would be a challenge to be secretary of a completely new organization. She met that challenge so well that, when she retired after six years we had to find four people to share the duties which she alone had carried out with such calm efficiency.

On that morning twenty people paid their subscriptions — while many others promised to join. After lunch I hurried to the bank to open our account with our first £25. The Committee held their first meeting and drew up the constitution. This stated that the aim of the Society was to help members to learn more about their plants and to gain skill in their care and cultivation.

A friend, who had come to the coffee morning, went that same evening to a dinner at which she sat next to a reporter from the local evening paper, to whom she confided: 'I was in at the birth of a new organization this morning,' and went on to give all the details. The reporter was intrigued, and asked next day for an interview. Her article roused a lot of interest, and when we held our first meeting in April we had a hundred members, to whom we were able to present a membership card and completed programme for the year.

In order to produce that card in such record time Mrs. Smythe, the Secretary, and I spent hours telephoning and writing letters, visiting prospective halls, arranging speakers, outings and open gardens, and so on.

Meetings were to start punctually at 2.30 p.m., and announcements would be kept to a minimum, taking no longer than three to four minutes. Like this we hoped members would learn to arrive on time, and mothers who had to collect children from school at 4 p.m. would be able to enjoy the whole lecture. We acquired a notice board which gave all the details of outings, discounts on bulbs, seeds and other items — which if recited from the platform would have lengthened the proceedings, and created an atmosphere of stunned boredom most unpropitious for the speaker. Disastrously, at the very first meeting — with all those eager members, the press and guests from local specialist societies — the speaker was late! I extended my welcoming remarks to cover the next ghastly, interminable quarter of an hour, trying to look calm and in full command of the situation. Meanwhile the Secretary frantically searched for the Warden of the Community Centre where the meeting was held. His office, which contained the only telephone, was locked. From my unenviably elevated isolation on the platform I could see other members of the Committee outside anxiously scanning the roads in case the speaker had misread our map and taken a wrong turning. I prayed that none of the audience realized that all this hand-wringing activity was going on. Suddenly he arrived — bright and cheerful, and hoped he hadn't kept us waiting, but he knew how we ladies liked to have a chat at the beginning of our meetings! My welcoming smile did not even quiver, it had set so firmly that I felt sure it would have to be chipped away when I got home.

Then came the next horror — the plug on his projector did not fit into *any* of the sockets we had provided on the board prepared for this type of emergency. Another five minutes went by while the Warden produced and fixed another plug. Trembling I took my seat as the lights went out and we waited for the first slide. It flashed on the screen and then all went black — the bulb had gone! Fortunately he had a spare, but my hopes of establishing a reputation for punctuality were in ruins as the talk got under way at 3 p.m. Finally, I felt quite crushed by catastrophe when it became obvious that his subject was not the one advertised, and was much too elementary and general for this eclectic gathering. Everyone present was very kind, but I was quite sure the whole scheme for a horticultural society was doomed. We must have appeared inept, inefficient, bungling and uninformed. At our next committee meeting all was woe and desolation, and we looked for means of avoiding such an incredible series of misfortunes in the future. We planned to buy our own projector as soon as possible, to ask all speakers to arrive no later than 2.15 p.m. making it quite clear that our 'business' at the beginning was minimal, and that their talk could begin at 2.35 p.m. We have had occasional mishaps since — a speaker who did not arrive at all, bulbs which 'blew' during the showing of slides, some of which stuck and upset the automatic loading device on the new projector; speakers who could not be heard and so on — but never again such a concentration of calamities as at our first meeting.

The Society has flourished beyond all expectations — membership is almost two hundred — and although a few resign or move away each year, there are always a compensating number of new members to fill their places. We have a small, but comprehensive library of gardening books contained in two excellent bookcases on wheels given by one of our founder members. These are locked and kept at the Community Centre, and members can borrow two books per month. By another piece of good fortune one member had been a librarian before her marriage, and successfully steered this enterprise through its first hazardous days when there were not enough books to permit any to be overdue for more than one meeting. We have a special library committee, who draw up a list of books and scan the reviews to keep us up to date. The Treasurer allows us a sum from funds, and coffee mornings, 'bring and buys', as well as gifts, do the rest.

The exhibition table has been a source of interest and instruction to all of us. A band of experienced and knowledgeable gardeners are in charge of this feature, and every month they are surrounded by keen, questioning women wanting to know all about the specimens contributed by fellow members. We ask those bringing exhibits to label them carefully and give us any particulars, such as source of supply, height, position in the garden, and so on. Even in the depth of winter we have had most interesting collections of plants culled from garden and greenhouse.

It is particularly of value to beginners who see plants that were previously unknown or merely names in a catalogue, and who then realize that these can be grown locally. They have an opportunity to talk to the people who grow them, and find out all the required growing conditions and possible hazards.

The women who look after the Sales Table are absolute heroines, They arrive for monthly meetings at 1.30, carrying all the stock, and their own offerings for the table. They receive and price all the plants, seedlings and cuttings as members bring them, and the first eager beavers usually arrive at 1.45 p.m. Then they remain calm, cheerful and extremely busy during the crescendo of greedy gardeners in search of bargains.

Bargains they find too, each month, for our policy has always been to charge only a nominal sum for the items brought for the Sales Table. In fact some members grumble occasionally that higher prices are not asked for some of the choicer plants they have given. But we have remained adamant that the Society exists to provide opportunities and amenities like this for its members. It is not a money-making organization, although gardeners' charities do benefit from our Open Gardens.

Sometimes people want to get rid of expensive plants that are either unsuitable for their particular gardens, or which they wish to oust to make room for new favourites. We provide a service whereby they can enter a description of such a plant and the price wanted in a 'Surplus to Requirements' book. The transaction is then conducted between the members concerned, and is not the responsibility of the Sales Table helpers.

There is a large card index for 'Wanted' and 'Available' plants. This enables members collecting particular genera to complete their collections, and exchange their surplus with gardeners who share their special interest. Such treasures might be snapped up by the undiscerning or unappreciative were they placed on the table for general sale.

In my conservatory there is a lovely variety of *Begonia semperflorens* with dark red leaves and double pink flowers. I have forgotten its name, but shall always remember the occasion on which I acquired it. The speaker, to illustrate his excellent talk on cool greenhouses, had brought a number of beautifully grown plants, among which was a superb specimen of this begonia. With justifiable pride he told us that it had taken him nine months to bring it to this stage of perfection. There were a number of slides shown as well, and afterwards we stood at the back of the hall having tea, when there was a crash. Horrified, we looked at the platform where one of the supports of our very tall screen had fallen as it was being dismantled, right across the table on which the plants stood. The beautiful begonia was smashed, and broken pieces lay all around. There was a terrible hush as we all gazed at the wreckage, and I searched my mind despairingly for something adequate to say to our speaker. But there were no words to cover such a dreadful mishap, and we went on gazing in silence, until he sighed and turned away. Then I heard myself babbling all sorts of fatuous apologies and condolences which I am sure in no way comforted or consoled him.

But even such a painfully embarrassing event had a touch of humour. The members stood around murmuring sympathy and stooping to pick up the poor crushed pieces which our guest wished to take home. Their better natures reprimanded their greedy gardeners' fingers which clawed covetously at each little piece of the plant. One could almost hear each person's own inner struggle: 'Just a tiny piece, no one would notice; if it grew I'd share it.' 'No, no, it would be unkind, he is so upset and yet he is being so gracious.' 'Give *all* the pieces to him . . . .' 'All . . . even that leaf cutting?' 'Yes — all.' Their better natures won; reluctantly and yet eager to help, and *so* full of sympathy, they relinguished every fragment. Virtue was rewarded, and many of us received tiny cuttings which we have grown on most carefully, glad that we need suffer no pangs of conscience about possessing this lovely plant. Each year I take fresh cuttings from mine, hoping to match the skill of that generous grower whose unhappy experience was my gain.

There were several men, keen gardeners, who had generously opened their gardens for us whom, as a gesture of gratitude, we sometimes invited to meetings when the speaker or subject was of particular interest to them. It seemed to the Committee a good idea to allow any men who wished, to become special members, as they would then feel free to come to whichever meeting they chose. The range of speakers and subjects offered by our Society is unique in the county and we felt it would be gracious to share our opportunities. A proposal was drawn up for the Annual General Meeting — that men be admitted on a non-voting basis, at the same time pointing out that probably not many men would be free in the afternoons and they would therefore be in the minority and the Society would continue to be run by women. It did not occur to us that anyone would object, and we felt that many members would be pleased to have their husbands join them at meetings. We proposed that there should be a special subscription for family membership, and looked forward to members' approbation, and congratulations on our happy idea. How wrong we were! One lady rang up before the meeting — she was ill and could not attend, but would I be sure that her disapproval was noted and her reasons for disapproving made known to the meeting. This I promised to do, feeling sure she was in a minority of one. But to our amazement one by one members stood up and voiced the strongest possible reasons for not admitting men to the Society.

'This society is a women's society. Men have plenty of their own.'

'If men join our Society it will be spoilt, we don't want them!'

'This Society is well run, well organized and we all enjoy it. We have excellent speakers, the best of whom are women — in a man's world this is an achievement.'

'I love my husband but I enjoy having this interest which he cannot share — after all I cannot share in all his interests.'

'The men wouldn't be happy till they had the vote.'

Of course there were some who spoke with equal vehemence for the motion. Even the shyest, most uncommunicative members had something to say. Up until now I had always regarded the business of the Annual General Meeting as a rather boring chore to be presented to a bunch of apathetic women who would much have preferred hearing about fertilizers, shrubs, herbaceous perennials or the like. But here they were, blood up, eyes flashing, every nerve aquiver — it was hilarious.

In the end we put it to the vote, and asked for a show of hands. After three re-counts demanded from the floor, we made all in favour stand and be counted; then all against. One lady was so excited she stood up both times! In the end we conceded defeat and the local paper carried the headline 'These green-fingered women vote to go it alone.' The absentee dissenter, whose views had been explained to the meeting, was interviewed at her home and quoted in full, with a photograph captioned 'She fought for women's rights.'

8

Plant associations

 AT FIRST I CONCENTRATED SO MUCH ON GETTING A succession of flowers and interest, that I neglected the importance of plant association, and was often bitterly disappointed by the effect of a plant standing awkwardly above, or ill at ease among, unsuitable neighbours. When the importance of good grouping became obvious, here was yet another fascinating aspect of this absorbing pastime that is not so much a hobby but more a way of life!

Grey and silver plants associate well with almost all colours, and give continuing interest for a very long period. The brilliant silver *Helichrysum angustifolium* and bushes of purple sage made a wonderful picture when the Pacific Coast irises, planted between them, came into flower. The irises were grown from seed, and the colours, therefore, had been unpredictable, but the whole range of delicate colouring provided by the orchid-like flowers was enhanced by this background, which itself continued to give pleasure all summer long, after the irises had faded. These Pacific Coast irises, and all the other species which I grew from seed, looked better in my opinion in this sort of mixed planting than in an iris bed. Probably iris specialists would not agree, and might be horrified to know that I used several of the species iris to enliven the May appearance of a bed of 'Red Favourite' roses.

Several very successful groupings were achieved quite fortuitously. *Alchemilla mollis*, with its soft grey-green leaves and sprays of lime-yellow flowers, seeded itself all round the edge of a bed containing rosemary and two sorts of lavender. The picture made when it was in flower was one of the most charming in the garden. In February the gaps in the bed were filled with *Crocus tomasinianus*; in June a small-flowered white cistus enlivened the bed, while in September *Sedum spectabile* 'Brilliant' gave another satisfying picture. But none of these planned plantings, for all their success, were as lovely as the achievement of the self-sown alchemilla. Strangely enough, two groups when I had planted *Alchemilla mollis* intentionally were not as successful as the accidental one first described. I had used it round clumps of *Alstroemeria chilensis* which, although fronted by the lovely purple of *Hebe* 'Autumn Glory', needed the lime yellow and soft green of *Alchemilla mollis* not only to show off their delicate pinks and yellows, but to soften their stiff stems, as well as hide the dying daffodil foliage. But the alchemilla remained spindly and poor, quite lacking the lustre of the self-sown plants.

The other mediocre result came when I used alternate groups of *Alchemilla mollis* and *Viola* 'Ardross Gem' to edge a narrow bed under a hedge, which also needed to camouflage its drooping bunches of dying daffodil foliage.

As a weed-smothering ploy I planted *Ajuga pyramidalis crispa* and *Geranium sanguineum lancastriense* under the rose 'Zéphirine Drouhin'. The leaves made an attractive combination, and I had not expected much bloom from the ground covers in such a shady position. But the bright blue spires of the ajuga and pale pink geraniums flowered profligately and made one of the most startlingly beautiful pictures I have ever seen, as they sparkled over the dark shiny leaves of the ajuga, and complemented and softened the overhanging roses.

As an expedient to save weeding round the base of a low yew hedge I again used ajuga — this time the one with cream variegation to the light green leaves. I was pleased at the effectiveness of the ground cover both at smothering weeds and lighting up the dark yew. But I was delighted when this ajuga, too, gave a bountiful display of clear blue flowers, turning that modest corner into something spectacular.

Brilliant colours need not always be present for a satisfying effect. In a shady corner, surrounded by the fresh hummocks of hepatica leaves, my solitary plant of *Helleborus viridis* displayed its bright green flowers, with further ground cover of *Vinca minor*. This pleasant little study in green was transformed when that lovely fern *Adiantum pedatum* unfurled its young copper-pink fronds in front of the hellebore. Even later, when the fronds turned green, the little picture was still attractive.

I had always been intrigued by the idea of a thyme path, and spent happy hours preparing such an aromatic walk across a very wide bed. I collected pieces and took cuttings not only from our garden, but from friends. I weeded and raked and levelled and added coarse sand, and then planted the thymes. There were several varieties of *Thymus serpyllum* as well as *T. pseudolanuginosus*, *T. herba-barona* and *T. doefleri*. I added a few *T.* 'Silver Posy' near the edge to add variety of height with one or two pieces of *Acaena buchananii*, *Cotula squalida* and *Antennaria dioica*, to fill the gaps more quickly. The first year after planting was not impressive. The plants had not grown together and constant hand weeding was needed to keep the unfilled gaps clear of unwanted guests, but with regular attention this was not an impossible task. Ownership of the piece of ground adjoining mine had just been transferred from one Local Government department to another, and during a sort of 'this-is-not-our-responsibility' interim, the rosebay willowherb grew in it, flowered, and seeded. Clouds of fluffy, airborne seeds marked its invasion of my property. In answer to my protests, someone was sent to scythe the plot. But it was too late to save me the hours of backbreaking labour spent in removing the willowherb from all parts of the garden, and particularly the half-grown thyme path, where they did not confine themselves to the empty patches, but fiendishly embedded themselves in the thyme itself. All that summer and all the next spring I was plagued with wave upon wave of them — every shower of rain produced an even thicker batch than the last, until I was ready to treat the whole area with paraquat. Eventually my persistence conquered. The thymes and other plants grew together and the reward was worth all the effort it had entailed. The varying colours of leaves and flowers blending and contrasting with occasional changes of height and type of foliage was delightful. Thyme does have an annoying habit of dying suddenly in the middle, but to repair such bald patches I kept a row of rooted cuttings in the frame.

Although neutral plants such as hostas and silvers can often

E   65

rescue an unfortunate colour combination from failure, there are times when it is better to admit defeat and start again. When I planted *Lilium* 'Enchantment' in front of the rose 'Paul's Scarlet', I tried to soften the impact of that clashing orange and scarlet, but nothing lessened the disaster. I was so ashamed of the way my lack of imagination ruined the beauty of each, that I eventually transplanted the lilies.

Geranium endressii, Hosta fortunei, Astrantia major and *Allium albopilosum* made a superb group round a half standard *Arbutus unedo*. No weeds troubled me in that corner. *Geranium endressii* produced its pink flowers almost continuously from May to September, the ghostly greenish-white, rose-flushed astrantias needed no staking, and grew well above the glaucus blue-green leaves of the hosta. Even after the silky metallic blue flowers of the allium had faded, the huge seed heads remained to add lightness to the group.

But successful plantings are, I am sure, highly individual to each garden, as well as to each gardener's taste. Well-tried and highly recommended plantings have not always succeeded with me although elsewhere I have admired them greatly. I planted the striking *Senecio ligularia* 'Desdemona' in front of a yew tree, and beside it, to contrast with its great orange daisies on their dark red stems, I planted a group of *Lobelia hybrida vedariensis*, which has rich dark violet flowers. The ligularia was a wonderful sight, because even without the flowers it is much sought after for its foliage. But it grew tall and strong at the expense of the lobelia, which needs a lot of moisture. Alas, the yew tree would only allow the bed to support one other handsome inmate besides itself, and the lobelia languished, sickly in the shade of its lusty neighbours.

Light, too, plays an important part in the success or failure of a particular planting. I once planted some *Linum narbonnense* beside the pink valerian, *Centranthus ruber* to mingle with *Artemisia pontica*. The bed faced south-west, and in the morning the sun slanted through the trees behind the grouping, touching the plants gently with a wonderful luminous effect. The linum looked dainty, mysterious, exquisite. In the afternoon when the sun shone harshly on the same planting, it looked undistinguished, even banal, and the linum's morning daintiness had become faded fatigue.

I am writing this chapter after the move to my fourth and, I hope, final garden, which is the subject of the last chapter. But it is appropriate to describe here a particularly pleasing association of plants which brings an elegance and range of colour to the August scene and which, for me, outshines the brilliance of any dahlias. The rose 'La Reine Victoria' with its soft pink cup-shaped blooms has *Lavandula* 'Twickel Purple' at its feet, and the agapanthus at its side rises from a crisply curling *Senecio cineraria*, and the smooth and cool *Othonnopsis cheirifolia*. Pink, purple, blue and silver — this could be an insipid cloying picture — but the clear red blooms of *Penstemon* 'Schönholzeri' give it accent, and bring it to life so that its gleaming lustre causes me to stop and gaze at it, many times a day.

I find penstemons a very satisfactory genus which gives a wide range of colour, with interesting well-shaped flowers in bloom for a very long period. Because one hears doubts expressed over their hardiness, I take batches of cuttings every year and overwinter them in the frame. They root easily and make good plants by the following season. But my original plant, *Penstemon* 'Garnet', has survived for three winters and one transplanting. Three others which I enjoy are 'Southgate Gem', 'Hewell's Pink Bedder', and 'Purple Bedder' — these last two both much more attractive than their names suggest. A friend has promised me a cutting of a white one, and I hope gradually to add a few more to this little collection — perhaps 'Hon. Edith Gibbs', cream flushed with pink, and *heterophyllus* 'True Blue'.

Books have been written which deal exhaustively with the art of planning and planting for year-long beauty in the garden, and what a very skilled art it is. It is too easy to concentrate on spring and summer flowers, to be left in autumn and winter with a desolate ragged patch whose appearance does nothing to relieve the gloomy cold. A clump of crocus in November, a spray of jasmine in December, the earliest hepatica in January — any of these are worth a borderful of the most colourful herbaceous plants in July. But even in mid-winter, grouping is still important. Each flower picture is much smaller, but should still be a picture even though some of the associated plants are brown skeletons. The evergreens which are the backbone of the winter garden can both protect and enhance the little groups of bulbs and sprays of bloom on such shrubs as *Viburnum farreri* and *Hamamelis mollis*. A word of warning here — let the treasures of the winter months be near the house, and easily accessible over dry ground. One particularly wet February, several of my friends were required to follow me over a very muddy piece of lawn to admire *Hepatica transsilvanica* in full bloom. I was rather put out because their raptures were so subdued, until I realized that their indoor thin shoes, inadequate for the occasion, were completely saturated. I, being the only one correctly shod for this small expedition, did not therefore, with cold wet feet, nurse fears of chills and rheumatism.

9

Walls and fences

 PERHAPS IT IS GREED THAT HAS ALWAYS MADE IT seem desirable to cover every wall and fence in the garden with just a few more climbers than space allows, or the experts recommend. Books on the subject had not only widened my knowledge but increased my avarice. After eleven years the front of the house, about 50 feet, counting the garage, was clothed by two *Clematis montana*, one *C. viticella*, one *C. macropetala*, *C.* 'The President'; climbing roses 'Maigold', 'Ena Harkness', 'Mme Butterfly', 'Daily Mail' and 'Mrs. Sam McGredy'; two pyracanthas, one *Chaenomeles* 'Pink Lady'; *Cotoneaster horizontalis*; all footed by two pink lace-cap hydrangeas, five hortensia hydrangeas, *Rosa* 'La Reine Victoria', and edged by London Pride and *Geranium dalmaticum* and small bulbs.

These grew and bloomed and beautified the tall gaunt house. Passers-by stopped to look and to admire. First came the two *Clematis montana*, one just a little earlier than the other, both pink. The morning sun touched the one on the garage, enhancing its colour and emphasizing the contrast between the delicate petals and the bronze tinted leaves. This beauty was equalled by the way the setting sun suffused both plants with a deep rose. Even this stage did not surpass the translucent porcelain look of the flowers in the brief period between sunset and dusk, when all colour is intensified. If I drove home at any time during the day, I used to stop in the road outside and gaze at them. I have seen other equally beautiful clematis, covering even larger areas, but to have these two growing so richly on my own house has been one of my greatest treasures.

After Martin died I remembered often his joking question: 'What do we do when all these things grow above the first-floor windows?' I have been finding out how difficult it is to do anything. I tried, but only half-heartedly, to obey pruning instructions for a montana that has outgrown its allotted space. 'Cut back, immediately after flowering', said the book. My weakness in discipline was repaid by stronger and longer growths — producing their wreaths of flowers on top of an increasingly gargantuan layer of old stems. To my despair I watched long shoots of 'Ena Harkness' and 'Mme Butterfly' vanish into the thicket, and produce their gorgeous blooms high up and almost unseen among the clematis foliage. 'Maigold', 'Daily Mail' and 'Mrs. Sam McGredy' responded to my efforts at bending the shoots horizontally, but there was no room to do this to the other two. I spent hours up the ladder tending the roses; they became thornier and I more despondent each season, as the battle loomed after the display of bloom was over.

Two years ago, I knew I must act quickly as soon as the montana had flowered. The unsightly mass of stems overhung the kitchen window, the roof and guttering of the porch, and was beginning to mask Sarah's bedroom window as well. That spring the flowering period was more gorgeous than ever, but was paid for very dearly in the three solid hours I spent aloft, when the last petal had fallen. I had to exceed the bounds of safety by at least five rungs of the ladder. I was scratched by hidden rose shoots and pierced by the thorns of the pyracantha. It was almost impossible to cut only unwanted growth, and beautiful new shoots fell to the secateurs. At last, dirty and completely exhausted, I stood by the mound of leaves and stems. The old bare wood of the skeleton of my montana looked ugly and mutilated. I could have cried with vexation. I had been too greedy, and planted too much, and had not been able to train and prune in an orderly fashion to the plants' best advantage. I got tired of hearing: 'What a shame about your lovely clematis — why did you do that to it?'

By the end of the summer new shoots had sprung unbelievably from the old twisted trunks and once again the walls were veiled with the promise of another glorious spring.

I had learnt my lesson. Overplanting is foolish — particularly on a wall. Nothing should be allowed to go so high as to be beyond easy maintenance. A week or two later as I struggled with *Rosa* 'Mrs. Sam McGredy' and *Clematis* 'The President', I almost forgot how lovely the copper coloured roses and vibrant purple clematis had looked together. 'The President' is one of my favourite clematis — its blooms are crisp and held proudly on their stems. But Mrs. Sam needed a much larger space than the one I had given her — round the front porch. Also, a little earlier, I only mentioned the plants on the front of my house. On the opposite side of the front door — at the side of the house — *Clematis* 'Nellie Moser' wandered through Mrs. Sam's great thorny branches to meet 'The President'. A prize of beauty to be paid for dearly in painful, and even dangerous maintenance.

'Maigold' was comparatively easy to keep within bounds, although its extreme thorniness made this an unpleasant task. Its repeat blooming is sparse compared with the first flush, which lives up to all the claims made for it in the catalogues. Its semi-double blooms are beautiful in form and colour, and the foliage is neat, luxurious and a lovely light green.

I planted yellow climbing roses with more unbridled affection than caution. 'Maigold' has formidable thorns, but the armature of 'Mermaid' is hooked and vicious. Our plant of this lovely single rose was planted in the autumn of 1962. The hard winter killed all its top growth. Martin pointed out that it did not have very much space for its roots — due to a subterranean air-raid shelter. I hoped its roots would accept the fact that they could not delve deep, and content themselves with lateral spread. By the end of the summer the only evidence of life was a sickly shoot, about 5 inches long. My common sense told me that this plant was dying — my optimism assured me it was beginning to live. For once my optimism was justified. Now, eight years later, 'Mermaid' sprawls all over the south-west side of the house, shading the roof of the conservatory, pushing through the roses beyond, and on its nearside throwing vigorous branches into the pink chestnut tree. It casts gloom over the dining-room and provides a succession of blooms just outside my bedroom window. It is almost evergreen, and although never smothered in bloom like 'Maigold', it is in flower all summer and late into autumn. The blooms measure at least

4 inches with a rich cluster of stamens, delicate fragrance and almost evergreen, glossy, medium green foliage. Its vigour and its thorns are its only drawbacks. I planted the modern shrub rose 'Gold Wings', also single and yellow, but it lacks the soul of 'Mermaid' and just misses being a rose to love.

At the other bay I planted *Rosa banksiae lutea*. This was a mistake planted for sentimental reasons. In that small but choice area I had already planted a magnolia (now ten years old, but not yet bloomed), *Rosa* 'Étoile d'Hollande' and *Clematis armandii*. It soon outstripped its companions and went even higher. I climbed perilously high after it, and spent a long tedious afternoon tying in the shoots horizontally. During its first three years it had one flower, but now, as I leave this third garden, it is covered in tiny pale yellow rosettes for the benefit of the new owners. The magnolia remains my gesture to posterity. 'Étoile d'Hollande', the first occupant of the little bed, was not a wise choice either. This was the warmest and most sheltered piece of wall in the garden. 'Étoile d'Hollande', also very vigorous, blooms early — many velvety red blooms with a glorious scent. But enjoyment of these precocious flowers is always short-lived, for the warmth which has encouraged their precocity, causes their petals to change colour and fall too rapidly. The thick strong new shoots, to produce later flowers, are difficult to train around the sitting-room window. Often after breaking several, I despaired, and allowed the others to grow and bloom against the pane, making the sitting-room as dark as the dining-room.

A little knowledge is always a dangerous thing — in the case of the *Magnolia grandiflora* it was, however, merely disappointing — I should have planted *M. g.* 'Exmouth' which would have produced its sculptured chalice-like blooms long before now.

'Goldfinch' — a charming little rose, was one of the very few good things we found in our garden: two spindly bushes were discovered under the evergreens, trees and weeds that edged the boundary. Given light, space and careful training they covered large areas of the fence. The only pruning needed each year was to cut out the dead and flowered wood, to make room for new growth. It is a pity that there is only one period of flower — no repeat blooming. But the golden-yellow rosettes which pale as they age, have a fugitive pervasive scent whose sweetness alone should guarantee this rose a place in any garden.

Another yellow climber which I grew successfully was 'Golden Showers'. Over the stump of a dying sorbus, which we killed because its heavy foliage had shaded our neighbour's garden, we grew this rose with *Clematis* 'Jackmanii Superba'. 'Golden Showers' really *is* a perpetual flowering climber. Not all the double plantings in the garden worked as well as this one, but it was too good to last. The stump died, and rotted and fell, leaving the rose and clematis floundering together. The idea of using a dead or dying tree as host for climbers is very attractive, but the difficulty of providing an alternative support after its demise is a risk not worth taking. This situation has arisen three times with different plants, which all suffered from the inevitable root disturbance.

Often roses I have planted as pillar roses have grown too vigorously to submit to being trained spirally round their support as instructed. One such was 'Guinée'. I decided that the pillar must become an arch. This proved far more difficult than would seem possible. In view of the collapse of the dying stumps of the last paragraph, I called in a local carpenter, and arranged that the rustic arch which he agreed to order for me should be firmly set in concrete. After twelve months' delay in manufacture and delivery he came back to explain and to re-measure. Six months later he telephoned to see if I still wanted the job done — by which time I had made a virtue of necessity and changed both my mind and method of pruning. The *Clematis* 'Mrs. Spencer Castle' makes an elegant foil for the beautifully formed 'Guinée' with its dark velvety red and wonderful perfume. Covering the rather ungainly lower stems are *Aster acris* and *Lavandula* 'Twickel Purple', and a tangle of *Potentilla potentilla* 'Miss Willmott' and old-fashioned laced pinks.

10

Gardening friendships, fellowship and gifts

 WHEN MY LOVE OF GARDENING BEGAN TO GROW AND claim more and more of my time, interest and energy, I felt very much an outsider. The esoteric conversation of gardeners, hoary in experience, made me long to break into their charmed circle, but left me in no doubt that I did not possess the necessary qualifications for entry. They spoke together of plants they grew and loved, of places where these plants flourished, of other gardeners who had better varieties or lesser-known species. They promised each other cuttings, and 'pieces', and it was obvious that when the transactions took place they would bring as much joy to both giver and recipients as the exchange of pearls beyond price.

When I managed to engage these idols of mine in conversation they were kind and helpful, but I knew that my elementary questions must bore them, and that the relationship would continue unsatisfactory as long as I had nothing to contribute. Much more than knowledge of plants gleaned from books was needed to pass muster here, and there is no short cut to experience. This is particularly true of gardening, which the Preacher's words so accurately describe: 'To everything there is a season, and a time to every purpose under heaven; a time to be born and a time to die; a time to plant and a time to pluck up that which is planted.'

Although some plants will stand a little forcing, their span of life is often short. But the hardiest, most long-lived plants mature slowly — and so it is with garden friendships and fellowship.

However, while it was necessary to have learnt something of plants before being able to enjoy full membership of the company of gardeners, it was equally necessary not to air this knowledge before disinterested friends. At first I wanted to share every new and fascinating piece of plant lore with all my friends and acquaintances, because I was so sure that the friendship we already enjoyed would thrive on such a delightful common enthusiasm. At quite an early stage in my unravelling of horticultural mysteries, a good, but brutally frank adviser warned me that I was in great danger of becoming a crashing bore; that such enthusiasm as mine was only felt by very few, and that my raptures over the white rose under discussion were better saved for that minority. Realizing how horribly true the criticism was, I swallowed my pride and took his advice!

Another of my enthusiasms which became almost an obsession was collecting cuttings, and this seems to me to be the place to talk about these a little.

I had read about hardwood and softwood cuttings, and when to take them. I had experimented with peat, peat and sand, sand, compost, compost with a layer of sand on top, vermiculite and hormone rooting powders. I became quite covetous and begged cuttings shamelessly from my friends, and indeed even on the claim of the slightest acquaintance, and took a spare polythene bag wherever I went just in case I should acquire another treasure to propagate.

When, after trying unsuccessfully to root average-sized cuttings of heather, I read that tip cuttings 1 to $1\frac{1}{2}$ inches long were required, in no time at all I had three seed boxes full of neat rows of such tiny pieces culled from our own and neighbouring gardens. This was in late summer, and by next spring a high proportion of the cuttings had rooted, and by the following year had made strong healthy little plants.

Whatever the gems being propagated, it is always a moment of awe and wonder to take a little cutting from its pot and see the first roots shooting from the callus at the base.

Not only is the propagation of plants an economic way of increasing both the quantity and variety of subjects in the garden, but it provides a fascinating study in itself. Growing plants from seed is one of the simplest methods, although it requires some patience. My plants of *Dictamnus albus* took nearly five years to mature fully, but this little-grown plant is one of the most satisfactory in my garden, and well worth the long period of waiting. It is difficult to obtain except from seed, and is not listed in many nurserymen's catalogues.

However, to be sure of propagating a particular variety true to form, vegetative propagation is a necessity. Cuttings form the readiest means of vegetative propagation. To quote the Royal Horticultural Society's *Dictionary*: 'a cutting may be defined as any portion of a plant, root, stem, bud, or leaf which is separated from the parent and induced to form roots of its own'. To cover fully the subject of cuttings and their treatment would take an entire book — so off to the library again!

Apart from rooting cuttings in pots covered with either polythene bags or little rigid plastic domes bought to fit the pots, I have found a simple plastic-covered 'box' one of the cheapest and most efficient propagators. A wooden, box-shaped frame 2 feet by 8 inches by 10 inches covered on five sides with polythene, is readily made by even so clumsy a craftsman as myself. I found it particularly useful for rows of heather tip cuttings, dwarf conifer cuttings and some of the smaller silver plants. I placed it over a prepared bed of peat and sand, or soil and sand, in a shady part of the garden, and had 90 per cent success with it.

Having tried all the rooting media from plain sand, and plain water, to special rooting composts and soilless composts like vermiculite, on the whole I found I had most success with a fifty-fifty mixture of peat and sand. On holiday, an ideal time for collecting cuttings, it was often difficult to keep them alive until I arrived home. I read of, and tried a method which involved sphagnum moss and a folded strip of polythene. The damp moss was placed in the envelope of polythene and cuttings inserted. On several occasions they rooted by the end of the holiday. This was a specially good method for acid-loving, ericaceous shrubs. At home I used sphagnum moss in pots with equal success. As soon as rooting took place cuttings were moved from the moss which contains no food for the new little plants. This of course applied also to cuttings rooted in peat and sand.

It is a truism that a pleasure shared is a pleasure multiplied and that the converse applies to sorrow. Often my joy in some particular flower was so great that I had to find some one *at once* to enjoy it with me. The first time my *Crocus chrysanthus* 'Blue Pearl' and 'Cream Beauty' opened wide in the winter sunshine I telephoned Martin at the office, and begged him to leave everything and come home before the sun moved and cast the crocus in shadow. He did indeed rush home at lunchtime, and found the beauty of the delicate reflexed petals an ample reward for such a valiant effort to please his spouse.

Again and again my daily help was called from her task to wonder with me at anything from a water lily to a lewisia, a climbing rose or a gentian. My daughter Jane, on her return from work, was taken to see each treasure newly unfolded since the previous tour of inspection. She was very appreciative and only once mounted a slight rebellion with: 'Mummy, your trillium is fabulous but that is the third time this afternoon you have called me to look at it!'

One of my hopes, when starting the Horticultural Society, was that members would now more easily find kindred spirits with whom to share their delight in their favourite plants, and also be able to lessen the burden of their failures by sharing those too. Two of my garden friendships had already been founded on a common interest in winter-flowering bulbs. During a conversation with these hitherto unknown fellow-members of the Flower Arranging Club, I told of my excitement that morning when my first *Iris histrioides major* bloomed. The previous evening the flowers had still been tightly furled like neat, dark blue parasols. My family, unused to such early-morning activity, were amazed when I leapt from my bed at first light and rushed to the window to see what progress the iris had made. There in the rough gravel under the window was the first brilliant blue flower, fully open, its companions still in bud. The two ladies to whom I told this tale had not seen *Iris histrioides major* before, and accepted without hesitation my invitation to 'Come home with me *now* and see.' The thrill of being able to share my flower with them, and their genuine and generous response turned a relatively minor event into a really important one. Both my new friends joined the Horticultural

Society and have made a great contribution to it. For all of us, the blooming of *Iris histrioides major* is no longer such an extraordinary happening, but we think of it with affection because it marked the beginning of a very happy association.

One further word about the intrepid iris — it stayed beautiful for nearly three weeks, although for one week of that period its chin was resting on frozen snow.

I have been most grateful to hear from members of the Horticultural Society how their longing for gardening friendship has been realized since they joined. Of all the benefits they have received through their membership this must be the greatest, though the least tangible. I have always felt it a privilege to be invited to see other people's gardens, with so much to be learnt of the owners themselves from their plants, adding another dimension to an already good relationship. At first I was more of a taker with, it seemed, nothing to give to these hospitable people so prodigal of both garden lore and plants. It was with great diffidence that we first invited some of the connoisseurs to see our garden. But how generous they were with praise where it was merited, and with what disarming kindness they proffered good advice. They made it easy to ask them on future occasions to come and tell us what to do about this or that horticultural dilemma. It was a moment of pride and genuine humility when we were first called upon to give *our* advice. The pride was the justifiable satisfaction at other's recognition of our success with a plant in face of their comparative failure. But the humility was an honest realization of the smallness of our achievement, relative to the enormous subject of which we were attempting to master just a fraction.

One year I distributed seven seedling plants of *Clematis armandii*, grown from Royal Horticultural Society surplus seed, and retained two for myself. The first plant to flower was grown by one of the seven who planted hers in a cool greenhouse, where it romped away and produced masses of scented blooms. Now the others, including my own, have grown and bloomed out of doors, and we have all agreed what a good all-round plant this is — with its lovely evergreen leaves, delicately russet new growth, and the exciting fat green buds that precede the clusters of white flowers. The sharing of pleasure and experience in growing *C. armandii* was all the more precious because they were *my* seedlings which had found such excellent foster parents. At last I had been able to give something worthwhile which I had raised myself.

A mutual friend is often indicated by the presence in someone's garden of one of her favourite plants.

'I see Mollie has given you some of her *Viola cornuta*.'

'Yes, and has she given you a cutting of this rose? — It has an interesting history. . . .'

So the happy summer afternoon is spent browsing round the garden of a friend, learning a little about one plant, able to give advice about another, promising a cutting, discovering a name, waiting while the hostess rushes off to find a polythene bag and a trowel so that she can share a treasure. All this epitomizes something whose price, like that of a virtuous woman, is above rubies, and which indeed cannot be bought: garden fellowship.

Water gardening and wall gardening

 FOR THE FIRST FEW SUMMERS IN OUR THIRD GARDEN we enjoyed playing tennis, much to the detriment of the surrounding borders. Gradually the demands of the garden and our pride in the improved results of our labours in it caused us to give up our sporting efforts. But the lawn retained its rectangular shape, and I disliked the straight lines of the whole garden layout, especially when seen from the top windows in winter. I would often take a welcome pause from bed-making, to ponder over ways in which the defects in design could be cured, taking into account permanent features such as the oak tree, yew trees and paved paths. I had no serious thoughts of changing it, but the planning made a pleasant diversion from household chores.

About seven months after Martin's death, I was feeling particularly downcast, and snow made it impossible to dispel my depression with the healing therapy of working in the garden. But even meditating on work to be done at some future date is a cheering occupation, and without pressure of immediate action, plans can be made at leisure with due reference to books and catalogues. I had admired a water garden made by a friend and her husband during the previous summer — perhaps a carefully placed pool would improve the garden scene, and creating it could be the sort of challenge which would bring fresh interest into a very desolate situation. The physical effort which it would require would leave me too exhausted to feel self-pitying and morose.

I put on my shabby old gardening coat, a rather extraordinary woollen hat, scarf and gloves and wellington boots, and went out in the snow to tread out a design for my pool, and surrounding bog garden. A glimpse of myself reflected in the conservatory window as I trudged round the lawn dragging my

8. Raised bed for small bulbs and alpines and silver plants requiring sharp drainage. Shown in its third year

9. The raised bed still looking cheerful in September after providing interest from January

feet to make a clear outline, was enough to raise my spirits a little. I looked ridiculous — and all is not lost if one can still laugh at oneself.

It needed several journeys to the top of the house to survey my pool design in relation to the rest of the garden, and back to the garden to enlarge it and alter the shape. It was a wonderful opportunity to plan this new garden feature, as the snow-covered lawn was my drawing board, and the distracting plants which disguised lack of balance and proportion during summer were gone. Only the enduring trees and shrubs and evergreen plants could be seen, and their value as permanent features and integral parts of the garden design could be assessed. From the top window it was obvious that a small pond would look ludicrous set in such a large expanse of lawn. Also, as the garden was quite flat, except for a bank beyond the oak tree, the area round the pond would need to be not only big enough, but high enough, to create a balance between the water feature and the rest of the garden.

All this rushing up and down stairs was very tiring but very exciting. The task ahead was going to be much bigger than I had at first thought, and would involve much more than merely digging a hole in the ground. By late afternoon it was too dark and too cold to go on tracing patterns in the snow, but I went off to the library and found several books on making ponds and bog gardens. Here was an aspect of gardening of which I knew absolutely nothing, and which promised to be of great interest. I spent all evening poring over the books and trying to transmit my snow drawings to paper. I could hardly wait for the thaw, so that I could start digging. It took exactly two months to dig the pond, and shape the resulting mound of excavated earth into terraced beds retained by shallow peat walls. My youngest son, Richard, offered to help dig, but after turning over two turves he remarked that it was much harder than it appeared, and thereafter confined his help to words of advice and encouragement from the side line.

I dug in all sorts of weather, soon reaching heavy clay. Then it rained, and the hole half-filled with water. But by the beginning of April the excavation was finished, and the pond, measuring 10 feet by 5, and 18 inches at its deepest part, had a ledge round three sides to take marginal and shallow-water plants.

A concrete lining was beyond my capability as well as being beyond my purse. Fibreglass was also too expensive, and so I had decided on a heavy plastic material specially recommended for the purpose. After using builders' sand, and then layers of newspaper to smooth over rough parts of the surface, I was ready to place the plastic liner in position. Unfortunately I chose a windy day, and as I could not bear to postpone this important part of the operation until calmer weather, the family had to help anchor the liner, and rescue odd sheets of newspaper which started blowing about all over the place.

At last my plastic-lined hole in the ground was full of water, and looked not at all like a garden pool, but exactly like a plastic-lined hole in the ground full of water. I consulted the book of instructions and refused to admit to any feelings of disappointment. By the beginning of July plants and fish were becoming established, and the waterside planting masked my not too successful attempts at cementing the edging stones in place.

The stones which edged the pond were flat pieces of Cotswold stone from a neighbour's dismantled rock garden. From the same heap we had brought many loads of sandstone to build a dry-stone wall. The peat garden faced north-west, but I had decided to have the south-east face retained by a dry-stone wall. This decision was partly dictated by economy — the stones were free, and I had already spent quite a lot on two loads of peat blocks. It did seem, however, that a wall facing south-east would provide an admirable home for a number of small sun-lovers. In this latter decision I was proved correct, but the former was yet another example of the practice of false economy. As the owner of the stone lived about three hundred yards down the road, I started by barrowing it. The surprised gaze of passers-by did not deter me from trundling my heavy barrow along the pavement, but I decided that time and labour would be reduced if it were transported by car. Three or four barrow-loads could be packed into the boot, and the strain on aching muscles was lessened. The family joined in, and Jane, who became particularly enthusiastic, managed, with assistance, to load an enormous rock into the car, completely ruining the suspension and eventually making it necessary for me to have a new car.

The book said that the building of a dry-stone wall should not be beyond the capability of the average handyman. To be an average handyman seemed a modest requirement, but I soon realized that my qualifications did not merit even that description. However, plants settled happily in this erection, and soon camouflaged its worst deformities. Sempervivums, lewisias and *Penstemon newberryi* grew and seeded themselves in the crevices, while *Genista lydia*, varieties of *Phlox subulata* and *P. douglasii*, *Lithospermum diffusum*, antennaria and *Veronica incana* jostled for their place on top. *Tanacetum densum amanum* — formerly *Chrysanthemum haradjanii* — was extremely happy on top of the wall, and its soft clumps of feathery white leaves made a delicate foil for the more colourful plants surrounding it. The top was also excellent for many of the tiny bulb species which had failed in other parts of the garden because larger plants had prevented the summer baking which they would have received in their natural habitat.

At first I despaired of ever covering the peat walls. I wrote to the author of an article in the Alpine Garden Society's *Journal*, who had described his very successful peat garden. He counselled patience, and assured me that once the plants established themselves they would spread very quickly. However, as usual, in my impatience I overplanted, and three years later was faced with a very difficult piece of disentangling and thinning.

Another mistake was in not realizing that the peat walls were so shallow that in summer they would cast very little shadow, and that therefore to plant shade-loving plants in them was rather a farce. I overcame that difficulty by planting dwarf evergreens where plants languished and shrivelled in the sun, but for the most part everything flourished in spite of a few rules being broken. The important thing was to provide cover for the peat blocks as quickly as possible to avoid their drying up completely and flaking. *Linnaea borealis* soon did this, but allowed other plants — *Myrtus nummularia*, *Pernettya tasmanica* and *Gaultheria itoana* to root into the peat blocks and bind them together. *Gentiana sino-ornata*, planted in pockets of almost pure peat, made sheets of blue in the autumn. *Gentiana acaulis*, which had previously eked out a miserable flowerless existence on a clay bank, when transplanted to the peat bed grew and bloomed prodigiously. When in its second year it produced fifty-one huge and perfect blooms I felt justified in inviting an Alpine Garden enthusiast, in whose shadow I trembled, to admire it. Admire it he did, and very enthusiastically too, although he assured me that informed sources considered that almost pure peat was not recognized as a desirable medium for growing *G. acaulis*; a rare occasion when I broke a rule and was successful!

Dwarf rhododendrons, species tulips, choice ericas, *Primula rosea*, *P. pulverulenta* — adiantum, cassiopes and phyllodoces — there seemed no end to the assortment of plants that would grow happily here. I often felt, as my peat garden matured, that were I only able to have a very small garden, it would take this form, as no other part of my half-acre gave such all-the-year round beauty and enjoyment.

But, talking of peat and dry-stone walls, I have omitted part of my pond saga. No sooner had I completed the planting of my pool than a friend arrived with two bucketfuls of pond plants, including two pink water lilies. I have never been able to look a gift horse in the mouth, and cannot bear to waste anything — particularly any growing thing, so I dug a second smaller pool about 6 feet by 4 feet and extended the peat and bog garden round it. This had not been part of my original plan, but viewed from the top window was certainly a great improvement.

The next step was to curve the borders at the sides of the garden, and three years later, when all the plants had matured, I had the satisfaction of knowing, without any self-deception, that now the whole garden layout was good, and that the water and peat garden, so laboriously created, was a well-furnished, well-balanced embellishment.

12

The conservatory

 WHEN WE ADDED A SMALL CONSERVATORY TO THE house it was mainly to give access to the garden from the sitting-room and dining-room without making either room draughty. But we made a new interest of this necessity, and entered on another previously unknown field of study. Having agreed that such an addition was required, we spent weeks deciding on the best place to site it. We sat in different chairs in the two rooms, imagining how it would look if it were in this or that position, calculating how much sun it would get if it were placed at the side of the house, whether it should be all glass, or brick and glass, where the door into the garden should be, and so on.

Finally all the decisions were taken: a 2-foot brick wall, large windows, casement with toplights and a very large glass pane in the centre front. The heating would be by thermostatically controlled, electric tubular heaters — and the builders started. It took an incredibly long time to complete — partly due to an unforeseen delay in the delivery of the glazing bars for the roof. I had expected it to be ready for plants in November, but it was early February before the first few pots were in position.

The months of waiting had not been wasted, however, as I had scoured the library for books on growing plants in stove houses, warm, cool and cold greenhouses, conservatories large and small. Economics dictated that we must confine our attention to cool greenhouse plants, but there were enough books on this branch of the subject to occupy all my spare time that winter. Formerly I had only been mildly interested in my friends' greenhouses, as I shared neither their knowledge of, nor enthusiasm for the plants in them. But since the plans for our little edifice had first been mooted, I had become an absolute nuisance to my nearest conservatory-owning friend and neighbour. With courtesy and patience — and not a little pride — she named her plants, explained their foibles, potted innumerable cuttings for me, and took me along to other owners of interesting collections under glass. These were all very strange to me, and I felt I should never learn about this new, fascinating range of subjects to be grown and tended when at last the builders had completed their task.

Martin had handed over complete care of the new hobby to me when he realized that tomatoes would have no place in our conservatory — and planned a little tomato house at the bottom of the garden for the next year, which would be his sole responsibility.

A wise gardener warned me against overcrowding the conservatory. Her vision of the over-abundance of plants my enthusiasm might lead me to cram into the available space was more accurate than that of the builder. He assured me that the tiled window ledge would be quite sufficient for all the plants I should want, and that he could visualize me relaxing in there, enjoying the sunshine, with just a couple of geraniums and a begonia or two. He was so wrong — it was one of the places where I relaxed least. There were always many chores — mostly pleasant — to be done to keep the scores of plants healthy and well groomed.

Once again I ignored the voice of experience and soon accumulated a great array of plants with a variety of growing requirements. Some were planted in the soil in the small un-paved area, and they grew very quickly. *Jasminum polyanthum* quickly reached the roof and soon needed wires stretching across the whole width of the conservatory to accommodate it. A small pink ivy-leaved pelargonium scrambled around the jasmine's feet and pushed numerous shoots through the mass of foliage across the wires. Although its main flowering season and greatest display was in summer, in February, when the jasmine was in full bloom, occasional heads of the rosy pink pelargonium peered through the clusters of sweetly scented white flowers. The whole house was perfumed with the jasmine, and there were enough flowers to cut arching sprays for friends as well as for my own flower arrangements.

After quite a long period of pleasure came the reckoning. The heavy tangle of spent blooms and flowered growth had to be cut out to allow next year's flowering shoots to develop — and also to allow some light to reach the plants beneath. In vain I tried to avoid cutting down the pelargonium, and many lovely pink buds fell with the jasmine. Then came the time of waiting for the unsightly amputated stems of both plants to reclothe themselves with fresh new leaves.

Undeterred by my experience of the dangers and disappointments of overcrowding in the garden outside, I went on to plant *Bougainvillea glabra* and *Hoya carnosa*. Both flowered well in their season, but required quite a lot of training and pruning. The hoya I kept in a pot, and never ceased to be delighted by the buds, looking as though dipped in wax, which opened into exquisite, fragrant flowers. The shoots were trained along the wires towards the jasmine, and the pendulous umbels were thus shown to greatest advantage. Then there were the fuchsias, pelargoniums, ferns, echeverias, begonias, campanulas and numbers of others.

Apart from the alarming spread of aphis and mealy bug, there was the enormous task of keeping so many plants watered, fed, re-potted as necessary, with dead flowers and leaves removed, and all arranged so as to display each to best advantage. I spent hours tending them, and periodically had to put everything outside so that the windows and paintwork and slatted shelving could be washed with disinfectant. Then I would inspect every pot and replace and re-group them all. This used to take over six hours, and although it was most exhausting, the pleasure of seeing the plants in their new positions in the clean and shining house made it worth every backbreaking minute. On locking up last thing at night we used to linger there, and savour the beauty of each leaf and flower. There was something so attractive in being able to enjoy this illuminated indoor garden when outside it was dark, and sometimes wet and cold too.

But the aphis and the mealy bug and the mildew had to be dealt with if our pleasure was to continue. So many plants in such a small place meant the rapid spread of pests and disease.

There were, I discovered, all sorts of problems with controlling these, as a cure which suited one group of plants might kill or scorch another, and how to avoid splashing the sensitive ones which lived beside, or even underneath an affected plant I wished to spray?

Once, I thought I had found a cure to suit all the inmates, and sprayed with it liberally before discovering that it had a dreadful smell — far more pervasive and lasting than that of jasmine or hoya. Not only the family, from whom bluntness was to be expected, but guests who normally displayed more finesse, were shocked into asking: 'What on earth is that awful smell?'

Mealy bug resisted all sprays and washes, and its spread showed by the increase of sooty mould on the leaves of many of my plants. At a question-time session at the Flower Club, I asked my question hopefully — how could I get rid of this pest? I felt quite crushed and humiliated when one very superior member of the panel echoed my question in horror, and then scathingly stated that I should *never* have permitted it to get into my greenhouse in the first place! Only my despair gave me courage to persist: 'But now that I have got it, how do I get rid of it?'

A less severe member of the panel took pity on me, and explained that I must painstakingly examine each plant, and paint each insect with a fine paintbrush dipped in methylated spirits. This would take a long time, but would be effective. She was right, and also taking to heart the first lady's stricture, I now always examine each new plant carefully. Sometimes a recurrence of the pest makes the meths. treatment necessary, and it never fails.

The enthusiasm of dedicated horticultural writers is, to me, more convincing than any other sort of proselytizing. So, when I read what a marvellous display *Schizanthus pinnatus* could make in the cold greenhouse I was very interested. We had seen some beautifully grown schizanthus at Chelsea that year, so I could not wait to get seed. The display achieved was certainly very good, if not as spectacular as the book and my memories of Chelsea had led me to expect. But the time and trouble involved were out of all proportion to the pleasure. The whole operation required a lot of pots and compost, and stakes and time and patience.

I potted the seedlings on from 3-inch to 5-inch to 8-inch pots, which needed watering, and feeding, and staking, and finally, arranging in a magnificent if rather precarious pyramid. I changed the pots around so that all should receive their share of light, giving prominence to the finest specimens, and varying the blend of colours. For the few weeks while the display lasted, my other duties were sadly neglected, because in the brief intervals when I was not tending the plants, I felt I must admire and enjoy the cause of all this labour. But when the last withered potful had been thrown on the compost heap I decided that in future so much energy must not be wasted on annuals under glass. In fact, many of the lessons learnt a few years previously by experience of growing in the open garden, were being repeated now for greenhouse subjects.

For a long time I would not grow Morning Glory, as I feared it might become a pestilent weed like its relative the common bindweed. But having been convinced that this was not likely, I grew two plants each, in three 10-inch pots. I watched with mounting excitement as the first bud swelled. Two mornings I rushed downstairs very early, hoping to find it fully open, but returned to bed disappointed. The third morning — there it was, beautiful brilliant blue. I could now appreciate the name 'Morning Glory' — as I had only previously seen the plant when the ephemeral blooms were on the wane in late afternoon. It was such a delicate, elegant glory; it looked so fragile, that I wanted to cry for its vulnerability. Such a moment of ecstasy had to be shared, so I roused my long-suffering husband and family, who, for once, were all as impressed as I. For the next two weeks we all rose early, in competition with each other to count the newly opened blooms, and see whose forecast, based on a count of the previous evening's buds, was correct. The peak was reached on the day when we counted seventy-five flowers. Then Richard pricked the bubble of our daily dawn excitement:

'It gets boring when there have been over seventy for more than three mornings running.'

It seemed that, for our family, the flower's glory had departed, and although I grew it again next year, only Sarah, my youngest child, bothered to count the newly open blooms each day, an occupation now regarded with some disdain by the other children.

My first visit to Australia started me on a search for Australian plants that could be grown successfully in pots under glass. I had success with *Eucalyptus cordata*, *E. globulus* and *Callistemon speciosus*, the scarlet Bottle Brush. The eucalyptus grew fast, but each year I cut them down and was rewarded by fresh silver-leaved shoots. Eventually, however, they became too large for manageable pots, and did not survive their first winter outside. This was no real heartbreak to me, becuase by now I had realized that pot plants are expendable, and if kept for too many seasons become tatty in spite of many re-pottings, as well as being rather a bore. So it was with the bottlebrush. There were eight of them, and although their flowers were spectacular, much pruning had made the plants an unattractive shape, (contrary to expectations on following pruning instructions). Also, for a long period in the summer they cluttered up the terrace, often suffering from lack of water, and when brought in for the winter, had grown beyond the bounds when they could live at peace with their neighbours. I presented them to friends with larger greenhouses than mine, feeling slightly guilty that my gifts would most likely eventually prove as much an embarrassment to them as they had become to me.

There is one clear-cut lesson to be learnt from this — to be ruthless in throwing out over-tired and worn-out plants. Otherwise a conservatory which should be full of beautiful growing things can easily deteriorate into a horticultural hospital for sickly or desiccated and stunted horrors.

13

Gardening with sentiment, but without sentimentality

 THE DEFINITIONS FROM VARIOUS DICTIONARIES WHICH
supply the basis for my antithesis are as follows:

Sentiment, a thought, view or mental tendency
derived from or characterized by emotion;
tendency to be swayed by feeling rather than reason; an
emotional disposition with reference to some object or class
of objects.

Sentimentality, mawkishly emotional; state of being sentimental to excess.

Translated into working terms for the garden it seems that
sentiment is permissible within the bounds of what is practical,
while sentimentality, which rules out practical and aesthetic
requirements, brings with it a lack of honesty which is
destructive.

Where feeling and emotion take over from good sense, the
garden suffers. Yet without any emotion the garden is a lifeless
uninspired place, where plants are not accorded the dignity
deserved by beautiful growing things.

For many years I carried in my mind the idealized picture
of an 'olde worlde' flower border, complete with lupins and
peonies, hollyhocks, delphiniums and phlox, such as is often
portrayed with much devotion, but little taste, on calendars
and embroidered cushions. During those years I suffered a
great deal of frustration in trying to grow this picturesque
collection of plants. Frustration because we lived in a district
where hollyhocks succumbed to rust; because the delphiniums
I had chosen were so tall that they broke in the first high wind,
however carefully staked, because the lupins invariably col-
lapsed as they reached perfection, when the flowers filled with
water in heavy rain. It was sentimental of me to go on trying,

until finally common sense made me realize that the type of planting I so longed to achieve was unsuitable for our light soil and for the draughty position of the border, backed by a high solid fence over which the wind rushed, breaking all the taller plants, and that even had I been successful this pretty cottage border would have been quite out of context in the garden of our three-storey town house.

In our very first garden I almost wept when Martin wanted to dig up the 'Dorothy Perkins' roses. They reminded me of my childhood, we must keep them, I insisted. But each year the memory of masses of pink and red roses garlanding pergolas and arches, receded a little further, as I sprayed the sad mildewed specimens with their few miserable blooms. My husband's good sense triumphed over my sentimentality, and they went on the bonfire.

It is often because of the memories they evoke that we love some of our plants, and we have to decide how far this emotional attachment should outweigh the more practical criteria of a plant's suitability for our gardens. The roses I have just described were so deformed by disease that they had become neither ornamental nor evocative. It was surely right that they should go.

Thirteen years ago, on a family picnic, we dug up a seedling rhododendron — the common purple *Rh. ponticum*. We planted it with care to commemorate Jane's last term at school, the picnic having preceded her final 'Open Day' celebrations. It was sentiment that made me dig it up this year to plant in my new and very small garden. It was sentiment that made Jane write from Australia: 'I wonder whether you will take the Overstone rhododendron, or will it be too big for the new garden.'

This sentiment is allowable, I think, because although common, the rhododendron is attractive, it has not yet outgrown its space, and in fact has helped give a much desired 'established' look to my new garden. When it is too large for its new home and begins to rob other more attractive inmates, I shall have to decide whether in retaining it I am not being excessively swayed by memory. Where sentiment enters into the choice of plant, the final and most basic question on the validity of the choice must be 'True or false?' I asked myself this question many times when choosing which well-loved plants to move to this new garden. The answer was 'False' when I thought of digging up a nameless hybrid perpetual rose which had already been in the rose bed many years when we bought the property. It had responded to Martin's careful pruning and feeding, and had given us all great pleasure for many weeks each summer. Because it had been one of Martin's favourite plants, I wanted to bring it and its attendant memories to my new home. But such a large bush, of such great age, would surely not survive the change. The answer, to leave it behind to bloom for many more years, was right, I am sure.

After reading a book about double primroses, I determined to build up a collection of these lovely flowers. Part of their attraction was based on the sentimental appeal of old varieties, found neglected in cottage gardens and saved by connoisseurs from being lost for ever. The chapter of quotations from famous poets singing praises of the little flowers, confirmed me in my addiction. A knowledgeable friend warned me that we did not live in primula country, and that doubles, which were notoriously difficult, were impossible in our area. Knowledgeable friends are often depressing although almost invariably right. But I have always found it easier to learn by the empirical approach, than by accepting good advice, so I ignored my highly respected friend's dictum and ordered my first modest assortment of doubles. They were 'Lilacina plena', 'Alba plena', 'Our Pat', 'Bon Accord Gem', and 'Marie Crousse'. I had read and re-read the chapter on varieties before making my choice, and had given even more careful study to the chapter on soil requirements. I had done everything possible to supply soil containing humus and ample supplies of plant food, and was ready to apply a yearly mulch, and divide the plants regularly. With great care I had found positions away from mature trees that would deprive the plants of moisture, but made sure that there would be the partial shade which the plants enjoyed. But I ignored the sentence which insisted that double primroses should only be grown where conditions were fully in their favour, and that even then, when grown in one environment in a particular soil, they might not survive when transplanted elsewhere.

Out of my fifteen plants I did not see more than a total of six flowers. Every day when I made my inspection, each plant looked a little smaller than before, and despite all efforts every one dwindled and died. Unwilling to admit defeat, I tried again, redoubling my attempts to provide a congenial home for these temperamental beauties. But I gave up completely after a visit to a garden in Northern Ireland one August. A long shady path was edged with primula-leaved plants as large as young cabbages. On my remarking on these, and asking their identity, my hostess told me that they were double primroses, which flourished and flowered profusely with practically no attention. Only then did I recognize my sentimental folly in trying to keep alive my few miserable plants. Earlier I called my love of them an addiction, and I am not completely cured of this even now. Just a picture of a well-grown plant in full bloom, or an ecstatic description in a horticultural journal is enough to resurrect a longing to try again, despite the experts and my own experience.

Single primroses have presented no such difficulties, and as well as the common primrose, *P.* 'Garryarde Guinevere', *altaica grandiflora* (now *P. vulgaris sibthorpi*, 'E. R. Janes', *Juliae* and of course 'Wanda', have grown well for me for many years. But my favourite amongst all these is not the rarest or most beautiful. It is a red primrose, smothered in yellow-eyed blooms every spring, which has been propagated vegetatively many times from the original plant. This was a Mothering Sunday gift from my eldest son Morris, when he was eight years old and a chorister in the parish church. Having sung at a wedding on the Saturday, he had received half a crown as reward for his 'overtime', and had spent it all on the red primrose growing in a pot. My feelings were very mixed when he proudly presented his gift, with a sidelong glance at his two younger brothers aged six and four. I was touched by his generous gesture, but angry with the shopkeeper for charging a little boy what in those days (fourteen years ago) seemed an outrageous sum. I was also a little dubious of Morris's motives, having noted that triumphant little glance at Charles and Richard — could it be intended as a proof of his superiority over them, not only in years but in ability to earn, and willingness to spend? The two younger boys looked crestfallen at not being able to match Morris's generosity, and it was a very delicate matter to thank him adequately, without making them feel inferior.

The little plant grew, and was divided and replanted until I had a whole row of 'Morris's primrose', and soon there were spare plants to give to my friends. It still grows strongly and brings gaiety and rich depth of colour to my garden in early spring, although Morris has now been dead for seven years.

For our family, *Lilium speciosum* will always be 'Morris's lily'. Inspired by his schoolmaster, a lily enthusiast, Morris, when he was twelve years old, saved up and bought a bulb of *Lilium speciosum*. Following the master's instructions and advice, he tended it with care. But when the lily bloomed Morris was in France on holiday. Each letter he wrote asked 'Has my lily flowered yet?' Our anxiety mounted daily as we knew he would be bitterly disappointed if it faded before his return. We put it in a cool and shady place; we watched over it; we watered it; we admired it and we photographed it. To our great relief, and Morris's great joy, it was still fresh and beautiful when he arrived home. Although that particular bulb has long since perished, I always grow this lily, sometimes in a pot, sometimes in the open ground.

Both the primrose and the lily I have spoken of deserve their place in the garden through their beauty and merit. Their sentimental associations make them even more precious to me, but were they insipid, worthless plants, those links with the past would be insufficient reason for including them and by so doing I would truly be gardening with sentimentality.

One summer, while on holiday, we visited a nearby country town on market day. This was a very different affair from the larger, more sophisticated market in Coventry. Farmers and their wives had brought their own produce for sale, vegetables, butter, bread, chickens, alive as well as ready for the oven. But the stall that really fascinated me was the tiny one at which a tall elderly woman was selling all sorts of things from her own garden. There were tomatoes, lettuces, little bundles of beans and carrots, eggs, jam and honey, and bunches of mint, thyme, parsley and sage. I could imagine her in her tiny cottage preparing all the vegetables, and packing the eggs into her basket. There was an old-fashioned bicycle propped against the stall, with a small trailer, and I wondered how many miles she had cycled along the winding narrow roads. Most interesting were the little plants, obviously freshly dug up that morning, and carefully labelled. Eager customers were questioning her on the various plants, and she patiently explained each one's needs, praised its virtues and listed its uses. Now and then she broke off to sell some eggs or some honey, or to promise an enquirer a particular kind of mint or thyme for the next week. Although it was almost noon and most of her wares were sold, I came away with a little pot of chamomile and a piece of *Campanula poscharskyana*. Both are very ordinary plants, and I could have obtained them quite easily nearer home, instead of tending them on the kitchen window ledge of our holiday cottage for a week, and adding them to our luggage for the return journey. But they have survived, and charm me anew each time I look at them, and remember that there are still places where everything is not mass-produced, and standardized, and prepackaged. They evoke the wholesome old-fashioned simplicity of that little market stall, which was the most refreshing experience of the holiday, and I am not ashamed to garden with that sort of sentiment.

10. View of the terraced peat bed in the fourth garden, giving all-the-year-round interest

11. *Malus* 'Golden Hornet' has bright yellow fruits which persist after the leaves have fallen

14

Once more with feeling

 FOR SIX YEARS AFTER MARTIN'S DEATH I WORKED hard to maintain the half-acre garden. None of my family was sufficiently interested to do more than mow the lawn occasionally, or help give the yew and laurel their annual trim. Periodically, too, daughter Jane would rake and burn the gigantic mass of garden prunings and rubbish, to which I added continually, without ever being able to make a successful bonfire. Each time she completed the operation, she took me to look at the beautifully clean site, with just a heap of glowing woodash in the centre, and begged me to learn about bonfire-making, so that never again would anyone be faced with such a mountainous mess. Somehow, I never did learn; in my impatience I tried to burn too much at once, and always ended up with an enormous, smoky half-charred foundation on which to place the next layer of rubbish.

It was a long time before I could bear to think of leaving the garden in which Martin and I had worked so hard together, and which had given us so much joy to compensate for all the backache. How could I possibly leave the scores of lovely plants, so evocative of happy occasions in our family life? New owners might enjoy their beauty, but the other dimension, that of memory, would be missing.

But on considering the annual tasks of hedge trimming, balancing on ladders to prune and tie in climbing roses and rampant clematis, cleaning out the pools, raking, scarifying and topdressing the lawn, I realized my ability and enthusiasm for them must diminish with the years in inverse proportion to the increased growth and vigour of the more demanding plants. If I had a smaller garden I could enjoy it, without worrying about the major jobs listed above. Eventually all my family would grow up and leave home — and I could not then be sure of the occasional bonfires made to burn, or other help given willingly, if sporadically, now.

As soon as the decision to move was taken, I began to make lists of all the beloved plants that would have to move with me. The garden was by now so overcrowded that I could take enough to fill my new plot, and still leave more plants behind than any new owner would wish for, or indeed cope with. The list, which I carried at all times just in case another 'must take' occurred to me, grew very long, and the digging up was completed long before my search for a new home.

The new garden is minute in comparison with its predecessor. But, having found it in the month of November, the time was ideal to start lifting the listed plants and placing them in pots, buckets, sacking, and boxes of sand, peat, soil or leaf-mould, ready to be transferred to their new quarters in February. I drew plans and sketches, and took endless measurements to convince myself that there would indeed be space to accommodate them. Because I intended to take them anyway, I *knew* they would fit in somehow. My friends were not so sanguine, and shook their heads sadly at what they considered reckless, wasteful folly. But at last I had acquired enough experience to give me confidence to persist in spite of others' disapproval and unbelief.

This chapter could be filled with a list and description of everything I have brought to my little cottage garden. It is more profitable, I feel, to indicate the types of plants, rather than give an inventory including each individual, and more important still, to try to give the reasons for my choice.

Although a negative approach makes an unhappy start, it simplified my task to eliminate at the outset the things I could *not* take. This excluded at once all the very large trees, shrubs and climbers, which to transplant would have been to destroy. All but a snowberry and a forsythia had been removed from the desolate patch at the cottage, so if it were to be given an established look, I must have some fairly tall trees and shrubs. Among the things I could not bear to leave were an eleven-year-old *Malus* 'Neville Copeman', two *Prunus* 'Amanogawa' (one 15 feet tall), four fairly young standards — *Acer platanoides*

'Drummondii', *Robinia pseudoacacia* 'Frisia', *Buddleia alternifolia*, and *Malus* 'Golden Hornet'. I chose the first three because I liked them and they provided strong emotional links with the past. But, like the rest of the list, they are beautiful, and in my opinion deserve their places entirely on merit.

Regretfully I left my Banksian rose — the cottage walls had no room for this rampant grower; but I was glad to leave the even more rampant 'Mermaid'. Her hooked thorns and enormouse shoots embraced the house far too strongly ever to be removed, and I did not intend to encage my new home with a replacement specimen of this vicious beauty. Old-fashioned roses would surely be the ones to look best in the new setting, but only 'Félicité et Perpétue', 'The Garland', and *Rosa gallica* 'Versicolor', often called 'Rosa Mundi', were of a size to be moved. At least so I thought, until a would-be purchaser and his wife walked round the garden displaying as much interest in it as a pair of wooden images at a banquet. As soon as they had gone I stormed back into the house, announcing furiously that such Philistines could not be allowed to possess *R*. 'La Reine Victoria' or 'Mme Pierre Oger'. I cut the roses back, and after preparing two enormous boxes of soil, dug them up. The former survived, the latter perished, and Philistines did not buy the house. So honour was satisfied all round at the expense of the unfortunate 'Mme Pierre Oger'.

Several subsequent Philistine tours of the garden roused my wrath again, and caused many plants not on the moving list to be added to the 'in transit' collection. Among these were a seven-year-old wisteria, a twelve-year-old *Acer japonicum* 'Aureum' and nine more clematis than the dozen I had planned to take.

There were several small collections of such plants as geraniums, hellebores, euphorbias and hostas, which I had built up gradually from various sources. A number of species of the first two on this list had been grown from Royal Horticultural Society surplus seed. It would be difficult and expensive to replace these, so one plant of each was dug up. I was astounded at the size of the roots of *Helleborus guttatus, H. abchasicus* and *H. orientalis*, and the amount of soil which had to be lifted with them in order to minimize disturbance. All the hellebores remained completely unperturbed by the upheaval, and produced masses of flowers while still in their boxes, continuing in bloom when eventually moved to their new home.

Although vacant possession of the cottage was given in February and the first shrubs and trees were planted then, we did not move until May, and even then quite a number of unfortunate plants had to remain in containers until mid July, when all the builder's materials were finally cleared away and the small paved area in front dug and surrounded by a low wall. *Clematis* 'Étoile Violette', at least five years old and with a very large root system, put out a lot of new growth in spring, but some time during June the sacking and earth surrounding it dried out, and the tender young shoots wilted and died. Full of remorse, I cut it back and placed it in a barrowful of peat, which I kept well watered. This, and a very dried up specimen of *Fuchsia* 'Mme Cornelissen' were the last to be planted. Their recovery was amazing, and by early September both were flowering profusely, continuing to do so until late October. 'Étoile Violette' settled down comfortably to overhang the wall, as if she had lived in the village all her life!

Although I had no intention of transporting any sickly plants to the cottage, I made exceptions in the case of several clematis which had survived for a number of years, wispy, frail and flowerless. If left behind, they would die anyway and there was just a chance that they might thrive in the new situation. One of these, *C.* 'Gipsy Queen', had had clematis wilt twice, and each time had thrown up new growth from the base. At first it had been planted in the lee of a large bush of *Rosa* 'Dr. Van Fleet', in the hope that the last few shell pink blooms of the rose would be enlivened by the purportedly free-flowering clematis, which would continue to give colour after the final rose petal had fallen. At the end of the third summer, when it was quite obvious that this delightful scheme was not going to succeed, I transplanted 'Gipsy Queen' to a moister position where she could retrieve the ignominy of previous failure by scrambling through a cut-leaved golden elder. Another three years passed, and still she showed no decent growth, nor yet a solitary bloom. For such a feeble plant to be alive at all denoted a will to live which should be rewarded by this last opportunity in a new home. If left behind, the new owners would surely put her on the bonfire, if in fact they even noticed her at all. I prepared the ground as thoroughly for the spindly little plant as for an aristocratic tree peony or expensively rare acer. Hers was to be the privilege, if she chose to exercise it, of flaunting her rich violet-purple blooms against the bright red hips of *Rosa moyesii*. My faith and optimism were rewarded, and on the last day of September, the first lovely flower on an elegant spray of fifteen buds opened to display the wonderful texture of her velvety sepals with silver reverse.

Ground-cover plants were another important category. It had been a long, slow business acquiring and growing them, and testing their qualities as weed-smotherers. Although most of them are easily obtainable from nurserymen, to buy a specimen of each vinca, ajuga, acaena, hedera and lamium would not only be costly, but dull. Part of the charm of my collection of these plants is in the little history attached to the occasion of each one's addition to the garden. The golden variegated *Vinca minor*, with large white flowers, dates from the time of my attendance at the practical day-release classes in horticulture with the Parks and Gardens students.

Two of my favourite ivies, *Hedera helix* 'Sagittifolia' and 'Buttercup', were given me by the late Mrs. Margery Fish when she was my guest after speaking at the Horticultural Society. The golden-leaved lamium came from a friend whose garden is a joy to remember; while a collected form of pulmonaria with pale blue flowers reminds me of the visit of another distinguished gardener, who enclosed his 'bread-and-butter' letter in an exciting parcel of day lilies and ground-cover plants.

For like reasons I chose a number of quite humble self-seeders, *Viola* 'Mrs. Dutton', *V. cornuta*, and *V. canadensis*, *Sisyrinchium bermudianum*, *S.* 'Mrs. Spivey', *S. striatum* and a little glaucus leaved silene with heads of bright magenta flowers. This last seeds itself harmlessly in paths and crevices, and cheers up dull corners in July and August. As a member of the Alpine Garden Society, when going on holiday I always note, from the Members' List, those hospitable people who welcome fellow-members of the Society to view their gardens by appointment. On such a visit, while on holiday in Northern Ireland, I was given some seed of the little silene which I had admired growing in an area of crazy paving. So my pleasure in the little flower is a double one — I enjoy it for its intrinsic worth, and also for the memory of that lovely Irish garden, which was the highlight of the holiday.

Digging up bulbs in November was rather like searching for uncharted treasure. The birds had removed quite a number of labels, and there was no top growth to guide me, but even so I managed to pot up a few of each of my favourites — although many were left behind. One of my best-loved daffodils is *Narcissus* 'Peeping Tom' — so gay and slender, which endures frost and snow when in bloom, and though left limp by them comes up smiling and fresh at the slightest hint of sunshine. Usually it stays in flower for at least three weeks. My original six bulbs had multiplied in seven years to form a large clump. I took some of these for myself and some for a friend, but when the remainder bloomed, the clump seemed larger than ever, with no gaps to show that it had been disturbed.

It had taken a long time to establish my *Cyclamen neapolitanum*, but they had eventually formed a carpet, the pink flowers of late August–September followed by the lovely marbled leaves; both, by their daintiness and elegance, make the larger pot-grown hybrids seem blowsy and vulgar. I remember reading in one of Mrs. Fish's books how she picked the little cyclamen seedlings 'from the intricate jungle on their mother's bosom' and raised whole colonies of healthy young plants. Thinking enviously: 'It's all very well for Mrs. Fish — but that sort of thing just doesn't happen to me,' I went out to look again at my own cyclamen patch. Perhaps I had not looked closely enough before, but what a thrill to find enough little seedlings to fill a large seed tray. Each succeeding year there were more, and I was able to bring several boxfuls of strong-growing plants to my new home. They have settled down without the slightest setback, and have already produced masses of flowers and leaves, and not a few seedlings.

All the rooted cuttings of silver plants in the frame were another section to be carefully potted up — I left behind only such rampant growers as *Artemisia ludoviciana* and 'Silver Queen', as such greedy spreaders could not be allowed to use valuable space. To give the new garden a good start I dug up one or two quite large lavenders — 'Twickel Purple' and *Lavandula lanata*, as well as *L. stoechas*, with its quaint flowers.

With herbaceous plants I meant to be quite ruthless — no plants that needed staking; no Michaelmas daisies to get mildew; only the best variety of any genus; only plants with attractive foliage as well as attractive flowers. In fact I checked the herbaceous perennials that I chose in Mr. Alan Bloom's book *Perennials for Trouble-free Gardening* — where he gives marks for 'longevity, sturdy upright growth, a long flowering period and shapeliness in growth . . . neatness in the plant itself, in and out of season, and adaptability'.

Plants with a low score could not be included where space was at a premium. There would be room for only one delphinium, and I chose to take a short variety named 'Blue Tit'. Although it only grows to 3 to 4 feet high, it is always wise to give it some support. The type of support I use is a patent one — a circle of wire mesh on top of three wire legs. Once in position the foliage soon hides the framework while the flower stems push through the little spaces provided and are held in a natural position — difficult to achieve with canes. The brush-wood method of staking — so beautifully executed in the Royal Horticultural Society's garden at Wisley and the Savill Garden at Windsor Great Park — is not always possible for people in towns, as the right sort of twigs are difficult to obtain there.

Rules are made to be broken, they say, and I had already broken my 'no plants that need support' rule. But later in July the strong blue accent of *D.* 'Blue Tit' was so obviously the right choice, that I congratulated myself on this infringement.

It was sad to have to leave my three enormous *Kniphofia* 'Mrs. E. M. Mills' which brought such a glorious burst of colour to the garden in late summer. But the smaller varieties which are more suitable for the new borders provide a colour range from flame through yellow, to the creamy white of *K.* 'Maid of

Orleans'. This last flowered continuously for at least eight weeks and is to my mind one of the most attractive of the 'pokers'.

One of the first things I had done on obtaining possession of the cottage's forlorn little piece of ground was to test the soil, using a home soil-testing kit which had been given me some months before. I did each of the tests several times, having no confidence in my ability to carry out even a minor scientific exercise like this with precision. According to my reading of the results, the soil was slightly acid to neutral with pH 6.0 and pH 7.0. This discovery solved the problem of what to do with the rubbish heap. I had debated for a long time whether to level it completely, or merely to remove the tins, broken glass and half-charred non-vegetative material, so that a peat bed could be built on the remaining rubble and soil. The latter course seemed the more attractive, and I set about building the shallow retaining walls with peat blocks. Thanks to the Women's Horticultural Society, not only the block, but also the granulated form, was available cheaply, so I was able to be generous in mixing peat with the soil in the little terraces. However, still not too happy about my accuracy in testing the soil's acidity, I dosed the area heavily with sulphate of ammonia, remembering that for every ounce of this watered in by the heavy rain that was falling, a corresponding weight of lime would be leached out of the soil, were any lime indeed present. This rather hit-or-miss scientific approach was very successful, and the dwarf rhododendrons, phyllodoces, cassiopes, ericas and gentians flourished and bloomed as never before without a trace of the lime-induced chlorosis, which had sometimes marred them previously.

During digging-up, waiting around in containers, being transported and transplanted, many plants lost their labels. In the majority of cases this did not matter, as evergreens and many deciduous plants were easily recognizable. The pots of bulbs were coming into flower when planted out, and so presented no problem. But I got into difficulties when trying to keep herbaceous colour groupings together — pinks shading to reds, blues through mauve to cerise, yellows and orangey reds together. I had to make a number of reshuffles when the plants came into bloom, but on the whole was pleasantly surprised at the pictures that resulted.

In the previous garden I had barely managed to keep the Cape figwort, *Phygelius capensis*, alive. It had been divided and transplanted many times, but had never done well, and had only flowered twice in six years. Being an optimist, I had hoped that with each new season and fresh site success would come, and come it did, but as the result of quite an unplanned operation. Among the more dejected looking boxes of shrubs standing among the builder's rubble, awaiting allocation to their place in the new garden, was something that looked like winter jasmine. It divided into three pieces which I pushed into empty spaces by the fence, wondering why I had brought along such a miserable specimen of such an easily grown shrub. The answer came in July, when the first scarlet tubular flowers showed my jasmine to be three strong healthy bushes of the phygelius, which gave a succession of bloom until September.

Quite a number of other plants benefited by the change of soil and situation, most notably *Euphorbia myrsinites*, *Hypericum* × *moserianum* 'Tricolor', *Salvia officinalis* 'Tricolor', *Fuchsia* 'Mme Cornelissen' and *F.* 'Mrs. Popple', *Convolvulus cneorum*, and most of the silvers. Another of my favourite hardy fuchsias, 'Tom Thumb', transplanted happily to the peat garden where it gives a welcome display of colour in August–September. Although it vanishes completely in winter, it never fails to reappear in late spring and makes a shapely little bush smothered in deep pink and mauve flowers.

Making this new little garden has been a most enjoyable task because at last I have enough experience to be able to plan the disposition of my plants with some assurance of success. Most of them are ones that I have now known and grown for a long time. Of course I have made mistakes — but they are of a minor nature and easily rectified. The mistakes I shall undoubtedly continue to make will add to my experience, which in its turn will help me to cope with them. Even in this small area there will be room to introduce new friends among the old, to build up collections of other genera, and add little rarities to the collections already begun. My taste in flowers may change as much in the future as it has done in the past, because one of the great joys of gardening as an art and a hobby is that it is never static, but always changing, developing, maturing and being renewed.

I have exchanged the challenge of a large garden for the entirely different challenge of a very small one. Instead of an unending struggle to keep the large plot under control, I face the problem of providing continuing interest throughout the year in an extremely limited area. If the garden becomes over-cluttered, it will be fussy and unattractive, but it could equally become boring for long periods of the year, because flowers of a particular season have been given an unequal share of space. Every plant must earn its place at the expense of the rejected ones with not enough to give in terms of beauty and interest. This means being sternly selective; I must be quite sure what sort of garden I want, and pursue that ideal with vigour, and a firm discipline in the choice of plants.

The builders working on my house murmured in amazement at the miracle of trees and shrubs so soon established in their new home. 'Instant gardening' they called it. How mistaken they were in their choice of phrase. It has taken more than half a lifetime to reach this stage in my gardener's odyssey — and I doubt very much whether the remainder of my span of years will give time enough to explore more than a little of the fascinating territory through which this enchanting, demanding journey may be made.

Quick-reference list of plants

Note: All these plants grew happily in soil with a *p*H of 6.5 —
the acid side of neutral — with the exception of the peat garden
plants where the soil was more acid.

Acaena buchananii — ground cover, prostrate rooting stems,
roundish, deeply toothed, whitish-green leaves ⅙th inch long.
Well-drained soil in rock garden or under the shade of trees.

Acer japonicum 'Aureum' — small tree or large bush with soft
yellow leaves. Slow growing; good, moist, well-drained soil.

A. platanoides 'Drummondii' — handsome, fast growing tree;
leaves vividly and liberally variegated with white. Good, moist,
well-drained soil.

Achillea millefolium 'Rose Queen' — mat-forming perennial with
flower stems 1–3 feet high; cerise-pink flowers in flattish corymbs.
Sunny, well-drained soil.

A. ptarmica 'The Pearl' — perennial, double white flowers in
corymbs; 2 feet tall, useful for cuttings; sunny position, well-
drained soil.

Adiantum pedatum — hardy fern. Dainty green fronds. Height
1½ feet. In variety *coloratus*, fronds are coral pink when young.

Agapanthus orientalis — evergreen, strap-like leaves. Flower stem
about 2 feet, with many-flowered umbel of blue. Light, rich
soil, full sun. Some moisture in growing period.

Ajuga pyramidalis crispa — perennial, 6 inches high, ground
cover, dark leaves with metallic lustre and spikes of blue
flowers. May–July. Moist shade.

A. reptans variegata — perennial. Good ground cover, 6 inches, especially in moist places. Greyish-green and cream leaves. Bright blue spikes of flowers May–July. Sunny position.

Alchemilla mollis — perennial; wavy edged, grey-green leaves, lime-yellow flowers June–July. 1–1½ feet high. Good ground cover. Sunny position, ordinary well-drained soil.

Allium albopilosum — bulb; 1½ feet high; flowers large, deep lilac umbels; attractive seed heads, flowering July. Sunny position, well-drained soil.

Alstroemeria chilensis — fleshy-rooted perennial, flowering stem 2–3 feet with umbels of blood-red or pink, lily-like flowers lined with yellow; flowering — August. Sunny position, light soil. Resents root disturbance and when growing from seed should be sown thinly and seedlings thinned out bodily without disturbing their roots.

Antennaria — plants for light, well-drained soil and useful in poorish spots in rock garden where grey, mat-forming plants are needed. Flowering May–June.
A. aprica — a very useful little ground cover, silver in summer but green in winter. Attractive little apricot-backed flowers.
A. dioica 'Rosea' — attractive, pale pink flowers.

Arbutus unedo — small evergreen tree with deep green leaves, bearing white pitcher-shaped flowers and strawberry-like fruits simultaneously in autumn. Deep, well-drained acid soil, but will tolerate some lime.

Armeria — perennials of compact, tufted habit with dense flower heads of varying shades of pink; will grow in very sunny situations, useful for edging.
A. caespitosa 'Bevan's Variety' — only 2 inches tall and has deep pink flowers May–June.
A. maritima 'Bloodstone' — flowers bright red, 6 inches tall, May–July.
A.m. 'Vindictive' — flowers vivid deep rose, 6 inches tall, May–July.

Artemisia pontica — shrubby perennial with silvery-grey, feathery foliage; good ground cover in dry, sunny situations.

Aster acris — perennial about 2 feet tall, erect and bushy, with many small, lilac-mauve flower heads. Flowering in ordinary soil, sunny situation, September.

Astrantia — perennials growing 2 feet high, flowering June–July in partial shade or sun in places where soil does not dry out. The leaves are deeply dissected, and the straight stems carry whorls of greenish-grey, rose-tinged flowers.

Bergenia — perennial plants with large, evergreen leaves, adaptable to sun and shade and almost any type of soil. Most species and varieties flower in early spring with short spikes of pink flowers.
B. 'Ballawley Hybrid' — very large leaves and 12-inch spikes of bright rose-red flowers.
B. cordifolia — most common, flowers reach about 10 inches above leaves.
B. 'Silberlicht' has 8-inch spikes of white flowers.

Bougainvillea glabra — vigorous showy climber for the cool greenhouse with large recurving spines. The flowers have large rosy bracts. This is the best species for growing in pots or as a larger specimen in a bed. Starts flowering while still small.

Buddleia alternifolia — large shrub, or can be trained into small standard tree; graceful arching branches with long, narrow, dark green leaves and wreathed in June with delicately fragrant lilac flowers.

Callistemon speciosus — Australian Bottle Brush — only hardy in the mildest districts, otherwise must be grown under glass. Medium sized shrub with narrow, pointed leaves and deep scarlet flowers.

Campanula poscharskyana — tufted perennial with 12-inch long, slender, spreading stems — semi-prostrate. Panicles of lavender-blue, wide-funnel-shaped flowers in May–June. Light soil, sun or partial shade.

Cassiope — a family of low, hardy, evergreen, heath-like shrubs with bell-like, white flowers in spring. All require lime-free, peaty soil and a cool position.

Centranthus ruber — perennial of 2–3 feet, dense red cymes of flowers freely produced. Very useful plant because it will grow in very dry positions or dry walls. Sun and ordinary soil. Naturalized in Britain.

Ceratostigma plumbaginoides — perennial with 1–1½-foot stems bearing brilliant purplish-blue heads of flowers. The leaves turn red in autumn. Flowers August–September in sunny position and light well-drained soil.

Chaenomeles 'Pink Lady' — a cultivar of the well-known flowering Japonica. A small-to-medium, rigid shrub with clear rose-pink flowers (darker in bud) flowering March–April. Ordinary soil — prefers sunny position.

Clematis — species and small flowering varieties.
C. armandii — handsome, evergreen variety, large, three-lobed, glossy green leaves, waxy white flowers in clusters in March and April. Grow on a sheltered wall. 20–30 feet. Needs no pruning.
C. 'Etoile Violette' — has a medium-sized, deep purple flower with yellow stamens. It flowers profusely through July and August, growing 12–20 feet. It likes a south, west or east aspect and should be pruned hard in February.
C. macropetala — masses of semi-double, nodding flowers of lavender-blue in April and May. Will grow 8–12 feet on any aspect. Needs no pruning.
C. montana rubens — valuable, fast-growing variety with deep pink flowers and bronzy foliage; ideal for covering north-facing walls, trees or unsightly buildings; 20–30 feet; May–June. No pruning unless it is necessary to restrict growth. Prune immediately after flowering.
C. viticella — a rapid grower with small, purple, saucer-shaped flowers hanging downward — July–September. Aspect east, south or west; 20–30 feet. Prune hard in February.

Convolvulus cneorum — a sub-shrub 1–3 feet high. Lanceolate leaves covered with silvery, silky hairs. Pale pink flowers in May. A beautiful half-hardy plant needing a hot, sunny place and well-drained soil.

Coronilla emerus — elegant hardy shrub of medium size with clusters of bright yellow, pea flowers in the leaf axils through the growing season. Sunny position — well-drained soil.

Cotoneaster horizontalis — low-growing, spreading shrub with 'herring-bone' patterned branches. Will cover north and east walls and banks. Rich autumn colour from berries and leaves. Deciduous.

Cotula squalida — hardy perennial, carpeting plant, spreads if noⱼ ept in check. Small, fern-like leaves. Useful for planting in pavement crevices or over spring bulbs. Any soil or position.

Crocus chrysanthus — there are many beautiful cultivars of this dainty, spring flowering species — the names 'Blue Pearl', 'Cream Beauty', 'Snow Bunting', to name just three, are accurately descriptive. They like light soil and an open, sunny situation so that they can show their full beauty by opening wide in the spring sunshine.
C. tomasinianus — is also spring flowering and one of the best for naturalizing as it spreads rapidly, although its cultivars do not. The colour range is pale lavender to red-purple.

Cyclamen neapolitanum — it is better to start with small plants than corms, which are sometimes difficult to establish. They like a well-drained soil and are happy under deciduous trees where, after flowering late August through September, they will carpet the ground with their beautiful marbled leaves during the winter. Flowers pink or white.

Daphne mezereum — deciduous, rounded bush up to 5 feet. The purple-red flowers cover the previous year's shoots in February and March, and are followed by poisonous, scarlet berries. Good loamy soil, moisture and good drainage. Thrives on limy soil.

Deutzia × elegantissima — easily cultivated, June flowering, deciduous shrub succeeding in all types of fertile soil. Sun or semi-shade. 4–5 feet high. Fragrant flowers tinted rose pink. Thin out and cut back old flowering shoots to within a few inches of old wood immediately after flowering.

Dictamnus albus — an excellent perennial easily grown in any garden soil; best in a fairly dry position and left undisturbed. Erect racemes of showy white or rose flowers rise above attractive dark green foliage. 2 feet high; needs no staking. Called 'Burning Bush' because volatile oil, produced in upper part of stem, will ignite on a hot still day if a match is held to it — and burn for a few seconds without damaging the plant.

Echinops ritro — Globe Thistle. Border perennial 3–4 feet tall, flowering July and August. Long, greyish, prickly foliage and upstanding, deep blue, globular flower heads on very stiff stems. Sunny position, well-drained soil.

Escallonia — valuable evergreen shrub with small, glossy leaves, flowering in July. Prune by cutting out old flowering growths immediately after flowering. Lime tolerant, drought resistant. Thrives in all types of well-drained soil in sunny situation.
E. 'Apple Blossom' — pink and white flowers smother the branches. About 4 feet, compact habit, slow growing.
E. 'Donard Radiance' — stronger growing, to about 7 feet. Compact habit. Larger, brilliant, soft rose-red, chalice-shaped flowers.

Eucalyptus cordata — dense-growing, tender, small tree with grey-silver leaves.
E. globulus — in mild districts a noble tree, but most usually seen as sparsely branched. Tender shrub. Leaves large, blue-green — almost silvery when young.

Europs acraeus — neat, rounded, evergreen shrub with silvery blue-grey leaves and bright yellow daisy flowers in June. Up to $1\frac{1}{2}$ feet high. Well-drained, sunny position.

Fritillaria imperialis — spring flowering bulb growing 3–4 feet with a circle of large, pendulous flowers at the top of the stem, surmounted by a green crown of leaves. There are varieties in yellow, orange and burnt-orange to maroon. Heavy but well-drained soil where the surface is rarely disturbed. Sunny position.

Fuchsia — many fuchsias are hardy and, although cut to the ground in winter, shoot up strongly again in spring. Flower freely through summer and autumn, thriving alike in sun or shade in any well-drained soil.
F. 'Madame Cornelissen' — has a red calyx and white petals.
F. 'Mrs. Popple' — has scarlet calyx and violet petals.
F. 'Tom Thumb' — dwarf bush 10–12 inches tall. Deep pink calyx and mauve petals.

Galanthus — snowdrops — like good, well-drained loam, full or partial shade, except for autumn or early winter flowering ones which need full sun.
G. elwesii — height 10 inches — tallest of all forms — with a large flower. January–March.
G. nivalis 'Atkinsii' — 6 inches; vigorous and large flowered; January–February.
G. n. 'Sarah Arnott' — 6 inches, February–March — the perfect all-purpose snowdrop.
G. n. viridapicis — 3 inches, February–March, green spots on outer segments.

Garrya elliptica — evergreen, leathery leaves and in the male form draped with 6–12-inch long, greyish-green catkins January–February. Useful for covering north or east facing walls. Succeeds in all types of well-drained soil. 9–10 feet.

Gaultheria itoana — an evergreen, creeping shrublet which forms dense mats of small leaves. Masses of bright red berries. Needs acid soil. Good as ground cover in slight shade.

Gentiana acaulis — perennial with large, rich blue, trumpet flowers in May, displayed over evergreen mats of foliage. Easily grown but does not always flower freely. Height 4 inches. Plant firmly and deeply in good rich loam in sun.
G. sino-ornata — late autumn flowering gentian; thick, grassy foliage covered with vivid blue flowers. Dislikes lime, full sun

and drought. Prefers light, well-drained soil, rich in peat or leafmould and shaded from the midday sun.

The following are not to be confused with the pelargoniums or geraniums grown in the greenhouse and for summer bedding.

Geranium dalmaticum — perennial, forming neat tufts of glossy foliage and deep rose-pink flowers of good substance. Easy in any good soil in sun; flowers June–July. Height 6 inches.

G. endressii — spreading perennial up to about 12 inches high. Light rose-pink flowers in summer and autumn. Good ground cover in sun or shade in any ordinary soil.

G. sanguineum lancastriense — neat, prostrate perennial, producing succession of saucer-shaped, rose-pink flowers delicately veined in red all summer. Height 4 inches. Sunny position, well-drained soil.

Hamamelis mollis — deciduous shrub of 10 feet or more. Large, softly hairy, rounded leaves; clusters of large, fragrant, golden-yellow flowers with strap-shaped petals from December until March on the naked branches. Sunny position in light, preferably acid, rich soil with some moisture during the growing season. Attractive, autumn-coloured foliage.

Hebe 'Autumn Glory' — a small, evergreen shrub of loose habit. Flowers of intense violet borne continuously in short, dense racemes in late summer and autumn. 2 feet high, needs well-drained soil and sunny or semi-shady position.

Hedera helix 'Sagittifolia' — a neat-growing form of the common ivy with arrowhead-shaped leaves with five lobes, the central lobe large and triangular. Good ground cover. Any soil or position.

H. h. 'Buttercup' — the best golden form of the common ivy. The rich yellow leaves become yellowish-green to pale green with age. Any soil or position.

Helichrysum angustifolium — perennial sub-shrub with a woody base and erect, slender, leafy shoots 8–15 inches tall, which are white with close, soft down. Leaves are $\frac{1}{2}$–1$\frac{1}{2}$ inches long, up to 1/20th inch wide, downy and white. June–August, yellow flower heads — but the plant's importance is in the bright silver foliage. It requires well-drained, light soil in full sun. Height up to 2 feet.

Helleborus abchasicus — nodding flowers, purple (or green within), 2½–3 inches across.

H. corsicus (syn. *H. argutifolius*) — a 3-foot-high, evergreen sub-shrub with leathery, green leaves and clusters of apple-green, cupped flowers in March and April. Rich, well-drained soil, in sun or semi shade, is required.

H. foetidus — sub-shrubby evergreen, 2 feet high, with dark green leaves divided into many finger-like segments. Large, many-flowered, green inflorescence — nodding, cup-shaped flowers from March until May. Rich, well-drained soil in semi-shade.

H. guttatus — white or pink flowers with red spots.

H. orientalis — 1-foot-high evergreen with large, leathery leaves and variable flowers — white, pink, purple or red. February–April. Rich, well-drained soil in semi-shade, topdress after flowering.

H. viridis — this hellebore is deciduous and bears its bright green, nodding, cup-shaped flowers in February. About 9 inches tall, the flowers over-topping the leaves. Likes semi-shade and a rich well-drained soil that does not dry out.

Hepatica — plants of tufted growth 6–8 inches high, remaining green through the winter but flowering before the new leaves appear in February–March. The anemone-like flowers cover the plant and vary from mauve to pale blue in the various species and forms. They enjoy semi-shade and leafy, rich, light soil.

Hosta — herbaceous perennials with handsome foliage, green, blue-green and variegated, with sprays of white or mauve, lily-like flowers which are often less important than the leaves. Any rich soil retaining moisture in semi or full shade. There are many species and varieties varying in height from 10 inches to 3 feet.

Hoya carnosa — an interesting, ornamental, climbing, evergreen plant for the cool greenhouse with leathery leaves and hanging umbels of wax-like, fragrant, pink flowers.

Hypericum × *moserianum* 'Tricolor' — dwarf shrub, 1½ feet high; leaves prettily variegated with green, white and pink; yellow flowers. Sunny, well-drained position.

Iris — Pacific Coast Hybrids — easily raised from seed and giving a wide range of delicate colours beautifully veined and marked. These beardless, rhizomatous irises form compact clumps of narrow, grass-like leaves and flower from the end of April through May. They like lightly shaded situations with well-drained, neutral to slightly acid soil.

Iris histrioides major — an excellent bulbous plant with large deep blue flowers with white spots on the falls, flowering in February in a well-drained sunny position. I have often known it bloom in mid-January.

Jasminum polyanthum — evergreen climber needing frost protection and therefore suitable for the cool greenhouse. Fern-like foliage and many-flowered panicles of very fragrant, white flowers in February–March, and occasionally thereafter.

Kniphofia 'Maid of Orleans' — tufted perennial with very long, narrow leaves and tall stems bearing 'torches' of ivory-blush flowers. Light, rich soil retaining moisture in the growing season, and a position in full sun.

Lamium maculatum 'Aureum' — golden-leaved, perennial ground cover making an excellent edging plant in moist soil and needing little trimming. Any soil or situation. 6–9 inches.

Lathyrus latifolius 'White Pearl' — white, everlasting pea. Climbing perennial flowering in August. Any soil, sunny situation.

Lavandula lanata – 1½–2-foot-high shrub — shoots and leaves white, with close wool, 3-inch-long spikes of very fragrant, bright violet flowers on 1–2-foot, slightly woolly stems.
L. stoechas — unusually shaded, purple flowers. 2 feet high.

L. 'Twickel Purple' — bright, deep purple flowers and grey foliage, 1½ feet.
All lavenders require full sun and a sandy, well-drained loam.

Leucojum aestivum — Summer Snowflake. 1–2 feet tall. Flowering in May, white with green tip, four or five flowers on each stem. Open, rich, moist soils — suitable for naturalizing like snowdrops.
L. vernum — Spring Snowflake. Large, white, bell-shaped flowers tipped with green. 6 inches high. Flowering in March. Similar requirements to *L. aestivum*.

Leucanthemum hosmariense — a 9-inch-high, bushy shrublet keeping its finely cut, steel-blue foliage in very good condition throughout the winter. White, marguerite-like flowers produced at any time of year with main flowering season in May. Any ordinary garden soil that does not puddle in times of thaw. Sunny position.

Lewisia — a family of about a dozen perennials with a rosette of narrow, fleshy leaves and showy flowers. Well-drained, sunny places in deep, rich soil; not always dependably hardy. Good for crevices in dry stone wall backed by good soil.

Lilium 'Enchantment' — a very vigorous, prolific and healthy lily growing 2–3 feet and flowering June–July with large, cup-shaped, upright flowers of intense orange-red, sixteen or more flowers per stem. Full sun or partial shade in good, well-drained soil to which leafmould or compost has been added.
L. speciosum — a lily which is excellent for either garden or greenhouse cultivation, flowering August–September on 3–4-foot stems. Flowers 3–5 inches long, white or suffused and spotted claret red, nodding with reflexed petals, very fragrant. Full sun or partial shade and same soil requirements as 'Enchantment'.

Linnaea borealis — a very pretty hardy trailing sub-shrubby evergreen with small rounded leaves, growing best in a rather shaded place, in moist, peaty soil. Tiny pink bell-shaped flowers are borne in pairs on erect 2-inch stems.

Linum narbonnense — 1½–2-foot perennial with narrow, glaucous leaves and panicles of large, blue flowers. May–July. Well-drained soil and sunny position.

Lithospermum diffusum — evergreen, prostrate sub-shrub up to 1 foot high, forming a broad mass. Deep blue flowers May–June. Dislikes lime, flourishes in sandy peat in full sun.

Lobelia hybrida vedariensis — 8-foot-high perennial with bright purple flowers in August–September. Likes rich, moist soil, well-sheltered in either shade or sun. Not reliably hardy.

Lychnis chalcedonica — 3½-foot-high perennial with bright scarlet flowers in corymbs, flowering July–September in any soil in a sunny position. Excellent in damp situations.

Macleaya cordata — a perennial growing to 7 feet with handsome, bronzy-green leaves, greyish underneath and large, many-flowered panicles of tiny, buff flowers. July–September. Sunny position at back of large border, but runs at the root and particularly in good soil is too invasive for the small garden.

Mahonia japonica — an evergreen, winter flowering shrub with terminal clusters of loosely held racemes of fragrant, lemon-yellow flowers. Height up to 6 feet. Semi-shade or sun. Any soil.

Malus 'Golden Hornet' — small tree with white flowers followed by profuse crop of small, bright yellow fruits which persist until late in the year. Sunny position, any soil.
M. 'Neville Copeman' — small tree with green leaves shaded purple throughout the summer. Flowers pink followed by conical, orange-red fruits. Sunny position, any soil.

Myrtus nummularia — the only hardy myrtle. A tiny, prostrate, evergreen shrublet, with wiry, reddish stems and white flowers in May or June followed by pink berries. Sheltered position in peat garden. Height 3 inches.

Othonnopsis cheirifolia — a pretty, spreading evergreen with glaucous leaves, 8–12 inches high. Light, well-drained soil in sunny position. Prune in late April.

Paeonia delavayi — this tree paeony grows to 6 feet in any well-drained soil in a sunny position and has single crimson-red flowers about 3½ inches across.

Penstemon — a perennial which prefers sun and needs good drainage. The border penstemons are not reliably hardy except in a mild winter, but root well from cuttings taken after flowering and overwintered in a frame. They provide a rich variety of colours from red and pink to purple and blue.
P. newberryi — a dwarf, shrubby plant for the rock garden with glaucous leaves and rosy-mauve flowers.

Pernettya tasmanica — a prostrate, cushion-like, creeping, ever-green shrub 3–6 inches tall. Red fruits in autumn. Sheltered position in the peat garden.

Phlox douglasii and forms — very close-growing mats studded thickly with starry flowers in May and June. Mossy foliage in summer, vanishing in winter. Well-drained soil, sunny position. Trim back after flowering to maintain compact habit. Succeeds in cold, exposed gardens where *P. subulata* forms do not.
P. subulata — also flowers in May and June; has similar requirements and showy flowers.

Phygelius capensis 'Coccineus' — shrub growing 4–6 feet tall in mild localities — higher against a wall. In colder areas it is apt to be cut to the ground in winter, when it can be treated as a herbaceous perennial. Panicles of tubular, scarlet flowers with yellow throats. Full sun, any type of well-drained soil.

Phyllodoce — a genus of hardy, heath-like, evergreen shrubs 4–9 inches high with bell-shaped flowers, preferring cool, peaty soil in a semi-shady position.

Physostegia virginiana — perennial with creeping roots which need some curbing. Glossy, dark, evergreen foliage and spikes of pretty, pink, tubular-lipped flowers. Height 2½–3 feet.

Potentilla nepalensis 'Miss Willmott' — perennial about 1½ feet high with inch-wide flowers of cherry-rose borne profusely from June to September. Sunny well-drained position. Seeds freely and comes reasonably true.

Primula 'E. R. Janes' — ideal primrose for the rock garden, the clusters of salmon-pink blooms almost completely cover the foliage in late March. Cool, rich soil.

P. 'Garryarde Guinevere' — a polyanthus with large heads of dusky pink, orange-eyed flowers over bronze foliage. Cool, rich soil — divide from time to time to keep healthy.

P. juliae — 3 inches high, bright purple. The well-known *P.* 'Wanda' is one of the many cultivars which have come from this species. Will survive dry periods in strong or heavy soil.

P. vulgaris — common primrose. There is a great diversity among these plants in colour, form, size of flower and habit. They also vary in their vigour and rate of growth. They need friable soil, well fortified with decayed farmyard manure if available — old mushroom-bed compost makes a good substitute. Peat and leaf-mould will help make a light soil moisture-retentive. The plants need dividing and replanting every two or three years. They also enjoy partial shade, i.e. beneath orchard or ornamental trees. The double-flowered forms belong here.

P. v. sibthorpii — blooms in mid March. Mauve-pink flowers are most prolific and of true primrose habit.

Prunus 'Amanogawa' — a small, columnar tree of erect habit with dense clusters of fragrant, semi-double, shell-pink flowers late April–mid May. Because of its non-spreading habit it is ideal for a small garden.

P. × *cistena* 'Crimson Dwarf' — this makes an excellent dwarf hedge up to 1½ feet high. Enjoy the white flowers in spring and then cut hard back. The plants will soon cover themselves in 1–1½-foot shoots with rich red leaves. Ordinary soil and a sunny position suit it.

Robinia pseudoacacia 'Frisia' — a small to medium-sized tree with dainty, pinnate leaves of deep golden-yellow which retain their brilliant colour from spring until autumn. Sun or semi-shade and a well-drained position are preferred.

Rosa banksiae lutea (1824) — vigorous climbing rose, 20 feet or more across. Needs a sunny wall to produce in May thornless clusters of pale yellow, double, rosette-like flowers.

R. 'Felicité et Perpétue' (1827) — very pretty, white rambler, nearly evergreen, with pompons of creamy white.

R. gallica 'Versicolor' (syn. 'Rosa Mundi') — this rose was known before the sixteenth century. It makes a neat 4-foot bush and carries masses of crimson flowers splashed and striped with blush-white in midsummer.

R. 'Guinée' — climbing hybrid tea (8–10 feet) with very dark velvety-red, well-shaped flowers which are heavily scented.

R. 'La Reine Victoria' (1872) — a Bourbon rose with beautiful, cup-shaped, rose-pink flowers, very fragrant. Erect shrub to 5 feet.

R. 'Mme Pierre Oger' — a sport of 'La Reine Victoria', differing only in its colour, which is a creamy blush.

R. moyesii — large shrub rose with attractive foliage; blood-crimson, single flowers followed by beautiful, large, flagon-shaped, red fruits.

R. 'The Garland' (1835) — this rambler (15 feet) has profuse clusters of small, double blooms, opening blush, fading to white. Fragrant and with small red hips.

Salvia officinalis 'Purpurascens' — Purple Sage. Should be pruned hard in April to maintain a neatly shaped bush 2-foot tall. Sunny position, well-drained soil.

S. o. 'Tricolor' — leaves variegated purple, pink and white. This is a very attractive small shrub. To 2 feet, it needs a sunny position and well-drained soil.

Santolina — these are small, bushy, hardy shrubs about 2 feet high, with finely cut, grey or silver foliage. They should be pruned in April to preserve a neat, rounded shape. The round, yellow flowers detract from the beauty of the plant and should be removed. Light, well-drained soil and full sunshine.

Schizanthus pinnatus — a very showy hardy annual with profuse flowers in a wide range of colours. Will flower in pots in spring in the cool greenhouse from seed sown the previous August or September.

Sedum spectabile 'Brilliant' — perennial with glaucous leaves on thick, fleshy stems 1–$1\frac{1}{2}$ feet high, with large flat corymbs of deep rose-pink flowers much loved by butterflies in September–October. Sunny, well-drained position.

Sempervivum — this is a very large family of succulent-rosette-forming, evergreen plants, attractive all the year round. They are particularly useful for rock crevices and dry-stone walls, and provide many-textured leaves in a wide range of colours from green to red.

Senecio cineraria (syn. *S. maritima*) — a sub-shrub with densely woolly-white, deeply cut leaves and yellow daisy flowers which should be removed. There are many named kinds ranging from 1½–2½ feet, with leaves of varying shape and degree of feltedness. They dislike winter damp and poor drainage, but can survive several seasons in a light, well-drained, sunny position.
S. greyi — an evergreen, grey-leaved shrub, white underneath, growing to 3–4 feet in sun or semi-shade in a well-drained position. The yellow daisy flowers may be removed as they are not very attractive. The shrub should be pruned hard in April.
S. ligularia 'Desdemona' — the main attraction of this handsome foliaged perennial (3–4 feet) is the large, dark green leaves, mahogany-red underneath. The plant will grow in semi-shade and likes some moisture. The bright, coarse, orange daisy flowers are quite showy.

Sidalcea 'Rose Queen' — this perennial grows 3–4 feet tall and likes a rich, deep soil in a sunny position. It carries rose-pink, mallow-like flowers on tapering spikes, over attractive, prettily-incised, green leaves.

Sisyrinchiums all like light, well-drained soil in a sunny position. They seed themselves rather freely.
Sisyrinchium bermudianum — grass-like leaves and clusters of blue flowers in May–June. To 8 inches.
S. 'Mrs. Spivey' — grass-like foliage and pure white flowers throughout the summer, on 6-inch stems.
S. striatum — resembles an iris in growth, but has straw-yellow, open flowers tightly packed on 2-foot spikes in June–July. Needs replanting every few years.

Tanacetum densum amanum — formerly *Chrysanthemum haradjanii*. A lovely carpeting perennial which will grow in any well-drained soil in a sunny position. The leaves are white and feathery looking, rather like tiny ostrich feathers. Height 6 inches. Does not flower every year. Flowers are poor — best cut off. Prune hard in late April to keep compact habit.

Thujopsis dolabrata — an attractive conifer with sprays of flattened scale-like green leaves, silver-backed. Makes a small tree or large shrub, broadly conical in shape. There is a dwarf form, smaller and more compact in all its parts.

Thymes all require a sunny position in light, well-drained soil.

Thymus doefleri — grey, hairy leaves, pink flowers.
T. herba-barona — delicious scent, rosy-mauve flowers; good cooked with beef.
T. pseudolanuginosus — grey, woolly leaves, mauve flowers.
T. serpyllum — aromatic, mat-forming perennial producing 1–3-inch flower spikes in June and July. There are many varieties with flowers ranging from dark purple to pale pink.
T. 'Silver Posy' — a silver-variegated little bush with mauve flowers, 6–9 inches tall. Evergreen, can be trimmed back after flowering in June.

Veronica incana — dark blue 3-inch spikes of flowers above neat mats of white foliage in summer. Requires sunny position and good drainage.

Viburnum carlesii — bushy, deciduous shrub 4–8 feet tall, liking a rich, moisture-retaining soil and sunny position. Leaves dull green. Very fragrant clusters of flowers in April–May, opening white from deep pink buds.
V. farreri (syn. *V. fragrans*) — medium to large deciduous shrub growing to 10 feet, with the same soil requirements as above. It bears small clusters of pale pink, sweetly scented flowers on the bare branches from November until February.

Vinca minor — there are very many forms of the lesser periwinkle with variegated leaves and different coloured flowers. Good ground cover — sun or shade. Good cover for small bulbs.

Viola 'Ardross Gem' — will grow in semi-shade and produces medium-sized, blue and gold flowers for a long season during the summer. 6 inches tall.

V. 'Mrs. Dutton' — tiny, pale yellow flowers, seeds freely and grows to 4 inches tall.

V. canadensis — medium-sized, white flowers tinged with mauve, May–July. Likes a moist soil and will grow in shade.

V. cornuta — will grow in sun or shade and flower nearly all summer. Flowers are about 1¼ inches long and light purple. There is a white form. Excellent for growing among roses. Seeds freely.

Index